MACOS BIG SUR USER G

The Ultimate Beginner's Manual To Using The Latest Marcos Big Sur Easily With Tips And Tricks

BY

FELIX O. COLLINS

Copyright © 2021 FELIX O. COLLINS

LEGAL NOTICE:

Contents

INTRODUCTION

macOS Big Sur was released at WWDC in June 2020. It is the latest version of macOS and was released on November 12. macOS Big Sur has a new look, and because of the huge expansion, Apple has expanded. to power on 11. macOS Big Sur is macOS 11.0.

Apple has introduced the biggest design update to macOS since the launch of Mac OS X with macOS Big Sur, which completely fixes everything from the corners of the window to the color and level icon design. The look is designed to make you feel comfortable and comfortable at the same time.

The glass window is lighter and cleaner, with more translucency and wider corners, the Dock is more glassy, the application icon has a new mouse tail style, and the menu bar has been redesigned. so as not to shrink the face. captures and integrates seamlessly with your knowledge, the sound system has been redesigned, and there are new signals in the toolbox, sides, and controls to provide clarity and balance between requests.

The buttons and controls of the application will be displayed when they are needed or missing when not in use so that the user can access the information properly, and the navigation menu will provide access to the custom configuration server, which owns the Wi-Fi, Bluetooth. as well as AirDrop controls, flash keyboard, no distractions, dark mode, volume level, etc.

The notification center has been redesigned with more notifications, compiled by iOS-style apps and apps, and can be organized into three different sizes. The new high-demand design offers a better arrangement of multiple glass windows and is easier to interact with on-demand.

Safari is faster than macOS Big Sur, saves power, and has a new start page that can be customized with wallpapers and selected elements (such as a "reading list" and the "iCloud signatures"). The Mac App Store is much easier to find extensions, and Apple has added a feature that makes it easier to install Chrome and

Firefox in Safari.

Apple has redesigned the tabs to make Safari's navigation faster by showing other areas on the chart and displaying images that show the taboos and threaten movements to give first previews of the page. Users can choose when and which sites to use extensions in Safari, thereby restricting site access.

Personalization has improved Safari's privacy. The display shows users which ones block Safari sites when visiting a site. Safari has a built-in translation option that can translate entire web pages into seven languages with a single click.

For passwords stored in the keychain, Apple will notify users by looking at the password. Password tracking is a protective feature that integrates strong keywords with other tools to identify users.

Currently, "Messages" is based on the iOS "Messages" app, which has many of the same controls as iOS 14, such as fixed conversations, @mentions, local replies, etc. Message format can be used on a Mac and supports the creation of Memoji and Memoji attachments.

The email app's search functionality has been improved to make it easier to find links, images, and keywords, and a new image option has been added in macOS, which makes it easier. and available in captions to send to friends and family Photo. . The photographer also uploads trending images and GIFs to add to emails.

Apple has redesigned the application for macOS Big Sur, including support for viewing, internal maps, and guides. These guides are lists of places of interest, restaurants, etc., created by trusted sources. The macOS map can be used to create bike and bike tours that can be sent to the iPhone, and ETA controls can be viewed on the Mac.

The "Photos" app has expanded its editing capabilities with a new retouch tool powered by machine learning, and Apple Music has been redesigned with a new "Listen to Now" feature, which also includes measuring with a reissued authority, interviews of artists, and a personalized party list.

With the Home app, the Home camera now supports visuals and workspace, AirPods are more flexible than ever, and Siri can answer new questions. up before.

With the new "App Privacy" feature, apps in the Mac App Store can help users better understand the privacy practices and information developers collect before choosing to drop the poloskalamu. Apple compares this feature to food labels for apps on the Mac App Store.

macOS Big Sur introduces fast updates that start in the background and end up being faster, making it easier to keep your Mac up to date, and including a cryptographically signed system to prevent hacking.

New features include using the history of trustees for the last 10 days, family support apps with subscriptions, quick style editing and improved search functions on Notes, the option to give reminders to people in the reminder program, improved Spotlight performance, and reports of how hard it is to rain and showers every minute in "weather".

macOS Big Sur was launched on November 12, 2020. It is a new free version of mac products of all products. If you're just getting started, take a closer look at the video below and then check out our list of 50 tips for a quick overview of what to consider when installing the update.

The Mac desktop

What is Mac's hard drive menu?

The navigation bar is displayed at the top of the Mac screen. Use the menus and icons in the menu bar to select commands, perform actions, and view status.

You can set the option to hide the cutout menu so that the menu bar is displayed when you move the cursor at the top of the screen. See how to change the Dock and menu options.

Apple directory

The Apple menu on the left side of the screen contains commands for performing tasks that you frequently perform, such as updating applications, unlocking system preferences, and locking. to the screen, and to disable the Mac. View information in the Apple directory?

Application directory

The application menu is in the Apple directory. The name of the application that you are going to use is displayed, followed by other menus, usually with common names such as a file, edit, type, or window. Each application has a "Help" list for easy access to information about how to use the application. Learn how to use the built-in help.

Each directory has orders, and many are available in the majority of requests. For example, the "Open" command is in the "File" menu. To learn more about the symbols used in keyboard shortcuts shown in menu commands, see the symbols displayed in the menu?

Status index

On the right side of the database, the menu is always displayed icons (sometimes called the status menu), which allow you to view the status of your Mac (e.g. flash level) or standard features (such as a flash keyboard.

For more information or options, click the status menu icon. For example, click "Wi-Fi" to see a list of available networks, or click "Show" to turn it to "Dark Mode" or "Night Shift" or off. You can choose what to show in the main menu.

To re-edit the status menu, click the Command key while dragging the images. To quickly clear the status menu, press the Command key while dragging the icon from the base menu.

Spotlights

If the Location icon appears on the menu bar, click the icon to search for items on the Mac and the web. Find out how to search using Spotlight.

control center

Click the server icon to open the control panel, where you can access frequently used functions, such as AirDrop, AirPlay, do not disturb, etc. See the central server.

Siri

If the Siri icon appears on the menu bar, click the icon and ask Siri to perform actions such as opening files or applications, or viewing information. on a Mac or the Internet. See Siri Usage.

Test Site

At the far right of the side menu, click on the date and time to open the "Notification Center", where you can see appointments, messages, weather, and information Others, and notifications will disappear over time. Check out the advertising center.

Search with Spotlight on Mac

Spotlight can help you quickly find applications, documents, and other files on your Mac. With Siri Ideas, you can get the latest news, sports statistics, weather conditions, and more. The flashlight can make the numbers and the changes for you.

Ask Siri. Sayings like: "How many centimeters in an inch?" Or "What kind of cook?" Learn how to ask Siri.

Looking for something

1. On a Mac, click the Spotlight icon on the menu bar (if displayed), or press the Command-Spacebar or press the Spotlight key (if there is a row of action keys on the keyboard).

You can drag the window to a position on the desktop

Tip: If the Sleep icon is not in the menu bar, please use the Dock & Menu Bar options to add it.

2. In the search field, type what you are looking for-the results will show up as you type.

Spotlight lists popular songs; click on a popular song to view and open it. Spotlight can point out various changes to your search; you can see these results in Spotlight or online.

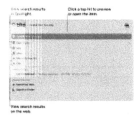

3. In conclusion, do any of the following:

- Show first look Pineapple. You may differ depending on the type of product chosen in the results. For example, select an application to see a list of files that have been recently opened, and then click on a file to open it. Or click the "Play" button to listen to a song.

- See expected results in Spotlight: Click on the product with the Spotlight icon.
- See expected results online: click on the item with the Safari icon.
- To open an object: double -click it. Or select the item and click Return.
- Locate the file on your Mac: select the file, and then click the Command key. The location of the file is shown below the preview.
- Copy the project: Drag the file to the desktop or Finder window.
- Find all the results on your Mac in Finder: Scroll down the results and click Search in Finder. Clear the results in the Finder, to see where the search results are empty.

During downtime, or if you do not reach the time limit set for the application in the "Timeout" options, the application icon will shrink and an hourglass icon will be displayed. See timeline.

Get scores and changes in Spotlight

You can enter mathematical terms, currencies, temperatures, and measurements into the Spotlight search field, and then edit or number the search field directly.

- Calculation: Enter a mathematical term, such as 956 * 23.94 or 2020/15.
- Currency conversion: Enter a currency, such as $ 100, 100 yen, or "300 kronor to the euro".

- Temperature adjustment: Enter the temperature, such as 98.8F, 32C, or "340K to F".
- Modification: Enter the measurement, such as 25 pounds, 54 yards, 23 stones, or "32 feet and meters".

Instructions: Click Press to display changes to the preview area.

You can remove specific labels, prints, or sensitive data (such as emails or messages) from Spotlight Search. See Spotlight Change options.

If you want Limelight to only search data on the Mac and not import results from the web, you can opt-out of Siri's suggestions for Spotlight.

Use Control Center on Mac

The Control Center on your Mac gives you quick access to key macOS system settings, such as volume, brightness, Wi-Fi, or "Do Not Disturb". You can modify the Control Center to add other items, such as accessibility shortcuts or fast user switching.

Use control center

1. On a Mac, tap "Control Center" in the list of the options bar.
2. Drag the slider (e.g. the "Volume" slider) or click the icon (e.g. the "AirDrop" icon). To see more options, click anywhere in the item, or click the arrow on the right.

For instance, in "Display", drag the slider to adjust the display brightness, or tap anywhere in "Display" to display controls to turn on or off "Dark Mode" and "Night Shift".

Tip: If you use an item frequently, you can drag it from the "Control Center" to the menu bar to make it easier to use here. To delete the item from the menu bar, hold down the Command key while dragging the item to the menu bar.

Custom control center

1. On Mac, select Apple menu> "System Preferences" and click "Dock & Menu Bar".
2. Click on a section in the sidebar to see items that are always in the Control Center or can be added.
   - Control Center: The items in this section always appear in the Control Center; you cannot delete them. Select an item in the sidebar to view its preview in the "Control Center" on the right.
   - Other modules: You can add the items in this section to the control center. Select an item in the sidebar, and then select the item's Show in the "Control Center" checkbox.

To include an item in the menu bar for faster access, select its Show in menu bar check box.

You cannot add items in the "Menu bar only" section to the control center.

Use Siri on Mac

Siri on Mac can help you complete everyday tasks, such as quickly answering questions, singing songs, etc. You can ask Siri, and Siri can either ask you ("meet at 9 o'clock" or "play soft music") or answer you ("what's the number in the game? last night?").

Siri can provide feedback on some programs before your request. For example, when you receive an invitation in an email or book a flight in Safari, Siri suggests adding it to your calendar.

Alternatively, when browsing the web, Siri can display related web pages.

Search Siri

If you set up Siri when you first set up your Mac, it may have turned up.

1. On a Mac, select the "Apple" menu> "System Prefers" and click "Siri".
2. Select "Enable Ask Siri" if it is not selected, then click "Enable."
3. If you are asked if you would like to improve Siri and dictation, please do any of the following:
   • Recording sharing: Click recording allows Apple to store voices based on the connection between Siri and Dictation from the Mac. Apple may take a look at the audio samples that have been submitted.
   • Do not share the recording: Click not immediately.

If you change your mind later and want to share or stop sharing the footage, select or uncheck the "Enhance Siri and Dictation" checkbox in the "Info and improvements" section. "Policy" options under "Security and Privacy. See how to change your privacy preferences.

Note: You can disable voice contacts at any time (for a specific period and less than six months), see Siri Clearance and Dictation history

4. Do any of the following:
   • Use "Hey Siri": If your Mac or dual AirPods support it, check the "Listen to" Hey Siri "box. Then you can say" Hey Siri "to start using Siri. Enable this option

and check "Lock After" Yes Siri Box in time ", you can use Siri even if your Mac is locked or asleep.

- Set up a keyboard shortcut: Click the "Keyboard Shortcut" pop-up menu, then choose a shortcut to request Siri and create your shortcut page.

Tip: If there is a "microphone" key in the action key row, you can press and hold to ask Siri or use a keyboard shortcut.

- Select Siri's voice mode: Click on the "language" pop-up menu and then select a language.) where Siri says.
- Hide Siri: Click "Off" on the "Voice Feedback" page - the response from Siri will be displayed in the Siri window, but will not be displayed.
- Add Siri to the hard drive directory: check the "Show Siri in the hard drive directory" box.

Ask Siri

1. Ask Siri on a Mac to do any of the following:
   - Press and hold the microphone key (if available in the business key row), or use the keyboard shortcut specified in Siri's preferences.

Note: Press and hold the microphone key to ask Siri. Press and release the microphone key to start dictation.

   - Click Siri in the hard drive menu. If it doesn't show up, you can add it using the Dock & Menu Bar options.
   - Click Siri on the keyboard (if your Mac has a touch screen).
   - Say "Hey Siri" (if Siri's options are available; this option is available if supported by your Mac or headset).

To make sure you can use Hey Siri on your device, check out Apple's support article for Apps that support "Hey Siri".

2. Ask Siri questions or fill out the tasks for you. Learn

how to use Siri.

Finish Siri

1. On a Mac, select the "Apple" menu> "System Prefers" and click "Siri".
2. Check the Enable Ask Siri box.

If you are the family organizer of a family sharing organization, you can set a "safe time" for your child and prevent access to Siri. Be aware of changing knowledge of the immune system and personal application preferences.

Use the Notification center on a Mac

In the Notification Library on Mac, you can download with missed notifications and use the app to see election times, birthdays, the weather, headlines, and more on the desktop.

Turn on or off the notification center on the Mac

On a Mac, do any of the subsequent:

- Open the notification center: press the date and time in the navigation bar, or use two fingers to swipe left from the right edge of the touchpad.
- To close the notification center: click anywhere on the desktop, click the date and time in the touchpad menu, or swipe the right edge of the touchpad with two fingers to the right.

Use the notifications server on a Mac

In the notification center, move the cursor over the notice, and then do one of the following:

- Add or break a group of notifications: If you aggregate messages from one program, multiple messages will be saved. To expand the stack and view all the notifications, click on each part of the top-notch message. To break down the stack, click Show Less.
- Do the action: Click the action. For example, click "Pause" in the announcement of the "Calendar" request, or click "Reply" in the announcement of the "Mail" request.

If there is a flower in the work area, click the flower for more options. For example, to use the "Messages" program to respond to a call, click the arrow next to "Reject" and select "Reply with a message."

- See more details: Click on the warning to open the item in the app. If you see an arrow to the right of the program name, click on the arrow to see the details in the notification.
- Change the billboard settings of an application: If an arrow appears to the right of the application name, click the arrow, click the "More" button, and then select an option:
  - Send slowly: notifications are not displayed in the right-hand corner on the screen or the lock screen (they are displayed in the notification center), and no sound is played when notifications are received.
  - Notification: Notifications are displayed in the upper right-hand corner of the screen and on the lock screen (and in the "Notification Center"), and sound when you receive a notification.
  - Hold: Do not take notice. To re-enable notifications for new applications, select the "Apple" menu> "System Prefers", click "Notifications", select the application on the left, and then click "Allow notifications" on the right).
  - Requirements to note: display the ad settings for

the "Advertise" options.

- Delete one or all notifications on the stack: Click the "Clear" or "Clear All" button.

Use the apps in Mac's Notification Center

On the ad server, do any of the following:

- See more details: Click anywhere on the app to open related preferences, applications, and web pages. For instance, click anywhere on the "Clock" widget to open the "Date and Time" options, or click anywhere on the "Recaps" widget to open the "Reminders" program.
- Delete a widget: While moving the cursor on the widget, press the Option key, and then click the "Delete" button.

Customize the ad server on a Mac

1. On a Mac, open the "Notification Center" and click "Edit Widget" below.
2. Do any of the following:
   - Find gadgets: Use the search engine to search for gadgets, or click on a section (such as the clock) to view available gadgets.
   - Add a gadget: When first previewing the widget, click the size (if available), move the cursor over the gadget in the preview, and click the Add button. The widget is added to the taskbar on the right.
   - Rearrange tools: in the work tool, drag the tool to another position.
   - Correct Widgets: In the widgets, move the arrow over the widget ("Correct Widget" appears under its name), and click anywhere on the widget. Add a widget to display settings that you can customize, for example, you can change the list displayed in the "Reminder" widget. When you are ready, click "Finish".
   - Add a widget: in the app, press the Control key and

click a widget, then select another size.

- Delete task tool: Move the cursor on the task tool, then click the "Delete" button.

3. When you are ready, click "Do" at the bottom of the task-bar.

Understanding the Mac Desktop

At the top of the screen is the hard drive menu, and at the bottom is the Dock. It's in the middle of the table called. The table is where you work.

Change the desktop image

You can choose a new macOS desktop image - change the animation seamlessly around the day - or use your imagination. Personalize your desktop image.

Change the appearance of the desktop

You can choose a light or dark interface for the desktop interface, desktop image, Dock, and built-in applications. Look for light or dark.

Organize files on a desktop

If you want to put files on the desktop for easy use, you can use the stack to organize the files on one side of the table in the same way or other settings. When you add files to the table, only the files are added to the stack. Learn how to organize files in a repository.

See the window on the desk

If your desk has a lot of windows, you can use the Mission screen to quickly access the screen, or view an easy-to-use overview of all the general information on the screen, so it's easy to find a window you want. See See the glass windows and spaces of the Mission Control.

Use multiple desks

You can create other desktop locations to organize the activities on specific desktops. For example, you can navigate the email on one desktop while watching what is being used on another desktop, and you can easily switch between the two desks. You can customize each desktop to fit the task at hand. See It works in many places.

Use Dock on Mac

The Dock on the Mac desktop is a convenient place to access the apps and activities you use every day (like the launchpad and trash can).

The Dock can display up to three previously unused applications, as well as a repository for storing content you download from the Site. By default, the Dock is at the bottom edge of the screen, but you can set an option to display it on the left or right side of the screen.

Open the project in the Dock

In the Dock on a Mac, do any of the following:

- Open the application: Click the application icon. For example, to open the finder, click the Finder icon on the screen.
- Open the file in the application: Drag the file to the application icon. For example, to open a document you created with pages, drag the document to the Pages page in the Dock.
- Show items to the recipient: Hold down the Command key and click the item icon.
- Switch to the previous request and hide the current re-

quest: Hold down the Option key and click the current request icon.

- Switch to another application and hide the other applications: Your Choice-Command-Click the icon of the application you want to modify.

Do the other actions on the objects on the scale

In the Dock on a Mac, do any of the following:

- Display the task directory menu: Hold down the Control key and click an item to display its task menu, then select a task (e.g., "Show new news"), or Or click on the file name to open the file.
- Quit a request to quit: If a request leaves a response, press the Control key and click the request's icon, then select "Force Quit" (you may lose unsaved changes).).

Add, delete, or edit Dock items

On a Mac, do any of the following:

- Add Items to the Dock: Drag the application to the left (and above) of the line that separates reused applications. Drag files and folders to the right (or below) of a separate line separating previously used programs. The name of the item is entered in the Dock.

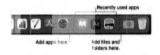

When you drag a file to the Dock, you can view it as a file. By default, the Dock comes with a download stack. Learn how to organize files in a repository.

- Remove an object from the Dock: Drag the object from the Dock until you see the octopus. Just delete the alias; leave the real thing on the Mac.

If you don't delete the application icon from the Dock, you can easily restore it (the application is available on the Mac). Open the application and display its icon in the new Dock.

Press the Control key and click the application icon, then select Options> Save Level.

- Rearrange items on the level: Drag items to a new location.

Tip: If you use Handoff, the Handoff icon of the app you are using on your iPhone, iPad, iPod touch, or Apple Watch will be displayed in the upper right corner of the Dock.

Customize dock

1. On a Mac, select the Apple menu> "System Prefers" and then click "Dock & Menu Bar" Prefers.
2. On the Dock & Menu Bar side of the page, change the options you want.

For example, you can change the way an item is displayed in the Dock, adjust its size, find it on the left or right side of the screen, or hide it.

To learn more about the options, click the "Help" button in the section.

Hint: Quickly adjust the size of the Dock, move the pointer to the dividing line in the Dock until a double arrow appears, then click and drag the pointer down or down. You can hold down the Control key and click the divider to get more actions from the menu bar.

You can use shortcuts to navigate to the Dock. Press Control-F3 (Control-Fn-F3 on Mac notebooks) to move to the Dock. Then use the left key and right key to move from one image to another. Click Enter to open a project.

The red button on the icon in the Dock indicates that you need to perform one or more actions on the application or Web preferences. For example, a red icon in the "Mail" icon in the Dock indicates that you have new emails to read.

Organize files in Finder on Mac

Finder is the foundation of Mac. The Finder sign looks like a smiling blue face. tap the sign in the Dock to open a Finder window.

You can use Windows Finder to organize up to everything on your Mac.

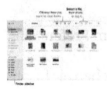

Find out what you have

Click on items in the Finder sidebar to see your files, applications, downloads, and more. For the page to be useful, customize it. For the Finder window to appear, display the "Preview" button.

Or, ask Siri to help you find what you need.

Ask Siri. Say this:

- Display me all the official papers called" fees "
- "Show files marked in red"
- "Show PDF files"

Learn how to ask Siri

Access everything from everywhere

You can use iCloud Drive to store files and folders in iCloud. You have the right to use them on any included devices with the same Apple ID.

Configure the use of files or labels

If you want to organize the files into archives, you can do so. Easily create new files on a document archive, desktop, or iCloud Drive.

You can label files and folders with keywords to make them easier to find.

Clean the messy desktop

Stacking helps you organize files in clean groups on the table. You can group groups by category, date, or label. When grouped by category, all the images are placed in one stack, the displays are placed in a stack, and so on. The new files you add go quickly to the stack — which should help you keep everything safe.

Choose your opinion

You can choose how to find items in the Finder window. For example, you don't need to view items in a list, the "Gallery" view allows you to view files and archives.

Send the file or archive

You can send a copy of a file or files directly from the Finder to a Mac, iPhone, or iPad. Click AirDrop on the landing page to get started. Use AirDrop to refer files to devices near you.

You can select files or folders in the Finder and click the "Share" button (or use the touchpad) to send them using "Mail", "Air-Drop", " Message ", etc. If you do not see the "Share" button, click the "More Toolbar Item" button at the bottom of the toolbar.

Sharing files and folders

You can share files or folders in iCloud Drive with other people who use iCloud. Select a file or folder in the Finder, click the "Share" button (or use the touchpad), and then select "Shared File" or "Shared Folder" to begin. If you do not see the "Share" button, click the "More Toolbar Item" button at the bottom of the toolbar. Use iCloud file sharing to share files and official papers with other iCloud users.

Synchronize information between Mac and other devices

You can connect your iPhone, iPad, or iPod touch to your Mac to transfer and update content between devices.

For example, when you attach a movie to your Mac, you can sync it with the iPhone and watch the movie on both devices.

You can link to content, including music, movies, movies, podcasts, books, and more. Take a look at the larger view that connects to the Mac and the device.

Use shortcuts to quickly complete tasks

You can use shortcuts to quickly perform common tasks. See Using macOS shortcuts.

Feature of macOS big sur

power of the present

The latest version of macOS Big Sur 11.2.3 was released to the public on March 8. macOS bug Sur 11.2.3 is an important WebKit security feature that fixes a vulnerability that could allow malicious system data to be compromised. create the code.

Apple has also rolled out 8 betas of the macOS Big Sur 11.3 update for developers and many beta testers.

macOS Big Sur 11.3 adds other standard options to Safari and provides new optimizations for the M1 Mac running iPhone and iPad apps. Includes support for the latest PlayStation 5 DualSense and Xbox Series X players, as well as improvements to memories, news, and Apple Music apps.

The code in macOS Big Sur 11.3 now features the "Optimize Battery Charging" feature to make sure Mac's battery is fully charged before the calendar event is arranged. The Mac will load 100% three hours before the start time of the calendar event.

The pre-configured installation is designed to preserve the life of the Mac chart by limiting the time to 100% of the Mac chart.

Redesign

macOS Big Sur gets a new version of macOS for the first time after Mac OS X, and Apple has introduced a new look but talked with emphasis on transparency, consistency, and visibility.

The workbench and side panels have been redesigned to fit well with each window, and the side panels have been raised to a very high level. The on-demand toolbox has no separate buttons, providing a cohesive and easy-to-use view across the entire system.

Windows is much simpler to design, has more rounded corners, and images in the application are made with animations and color changes. Apple has redesigned the icons for native applications, giving them a more mouse-like design, and there is an option to not remove the paint to darken the color.

In macOS Big Sur, there are some new features in the action boxes, sidebars, and buttons to create a click-to-click mode. Requests that share common routines (such as checking the mailbox in "Mail" or "Calendar") now have the same signal for inconsistency.

The updated application design can be found in the updated Dock, which has the same wide corners as Windows. The Dock has more glass than ever before and has a more refined design, so it can be combined with a desk.

Menu bar and control center

Now, at the top of the display, the solid base menu is translucent, which can be easily integrated with the desktop and can be hidden when not in use, like the solid base. The menu itself is easier to read, and the lines are larger.

The island icons and dropdown menus have been updated. It

should also be noted that the battery icon provides detailed information on the life of the remaining batteries. The battery usage history of the device is also provided in "System Prefers", and macOS Big Sur is included with the "optimized battery charge" feature added for the first time in macOS Catalina to extend the life of the device.

- How to disable chart view to be installed on macOS
- How to check the electrical health of Apple Silicon MacBook

The hard drive menu is the latest navigation center on the Mac, with quick access to Wi-Fi, Bluetooth, volume, display screen, keyboard layout, playing controls, and more. such as dark mode, true color, night shift, do not disturb, and AirPlay. The navigation center is dedicated, so you can set it to the most frequently used tasks at your fingertips.

Your favorite websites can be dragged and saved at the top of the site directory for quick access.

Sleeping paper

The desktop (the small pop-up window that pops up when you perform tasks such as printing and saving a document) has been redesigned on macOS Big Sur, and borders and restrictions have been removed. limit so that it cannot be seen. The table will be as black as the back and closer to the center of the application.

System sound

Traditional Mac voices have been redesigned and designed to be "comfortable". Each sound is created with a part of the original sound, so the sound is familiar, but at the same time new.

Apple has brought back the original music player that was released from the MacBook tablet in 2016.

Notification center

The notification center has been redesigned, and now notifications can be combined with apps in a single idea to give more information to the viewer.

Notifications are integrated by the app and have other chat features, so you don't have to open the app to perform tasks like update podcasts or reply to emails. Just click and hold the ho letterBe aware that new options are available.

The widget has been redesigned and is similar to the widget introduced in iOS 14. It can be customized in three sizes and comes with a widget menu to arrange it the way it suits your needs. There are several new tools available for applications such as Notes, Time Screen, and Podcasts.

You can find the three-page apps on the ad server on the Mac App Store.

New improvements and higher security

In addition to a clean and re-cleanup, macOS Big Sur also has a feature that allows new apps to start later and then finish quickly, so it doesn't take long to install new apps. Installing macOS Big Sur is a must for this feature, so macOS Big Sur is taking over the normal time.

This feature is supported by the newly integrated digital signage system in Big Sur, and the addition of a crime prevention platform. macOS Big Sur currently supports APFS Time Machine backup support, so with the addition of HFS +, you can use APFS backups to support your Mac.

Safari

Safari has a new start page that can be customized with a clip-board, and there are options to add favorites, frequently visited places, Siri ideas, reading lists, iCloud tabs, and more. and a per-sonalized presentation model.

Safari is faster and has better power than ever before. Compared to Chrome and Firefox, when it is loaded frequently on web-sites, it is 50% faster to load than Chrome, and the time when videos can be extended can be up to three hours.

Now, if you want to change the browser to take full advantage of the new features in Big Sur, you can download the history, book-marks, and passwords stored from Chrome and Safari.

Safari on macOS Big Sur supports HDR video and can be used with 4K HDR and Dolby Vision viewing from Netflix and You-Tube. Mac users can run Big Sur to watch content on 4K Netflix in Safari if they have a Mac of 2018 or later.

- How to add startup page layout to macOS Safari 14

Personal information

On the start page, the "Personal Information" gives you a sum-mary of the trackers that have been blocked from profiling you. If you click on the block bar on the side of the URL page, you can see the sites as well as the sites.

The privacy profile provides a list of all trackers on the site and the number of trackers that have been blocked, which then prevents sites from tracking your browsing activity on the Site. From the "personal information" menu option you can see how many trackers have been blocked in the last 30 days.

Tabs

Safari's tabs have been redesigned to allow you to see more

pages at the same time, and there's a new hover option that lets you hover over tabs to see a preview of the page. The pages have side icons, so you can see them at a glance.

- How to disable spyware in Safari on Mac

Extended name

There is a dedicated advertising section on the Mac App Store. Apple also includes support for the WebExtensions API. Developers can change the extensions designed for other browsers (such as Chrome, Edge, and Firefox) to a document that is compatible with Safari, and then add the extensions. about Safari users.

Looking to expand, Apple has added new privacy protections. You can choose the sites that can be extended, and you'll see a rule that offers broad rights to the extension.

Structural translation

Safari has a web browser that can translate up to seven languages with one click, so you can read the entire web page into another language without having to install an app.

Translations are available in English, Spanish, Chinese, French, German, Russian, and Portuguese.

Viewing password

For passwords stored in the keychain, Safari can now check to ensure that informants are not compromised. If the password drops, Safari will send you a message that you can change.

YouTube and Netflix in 4K

For the first time, macOS Big Sur supports 4K HDR YouTube videos in Safari, allowing you to watch higher-end videos in full resolution, unlimited at 1080p. It also supports Netflix's 4K HDR and Dolby Vision viewing, but Mac owners need a 2018 or later Mac with a T2 chip that can view content in 4K Netflix on Safari while it's running to Big Sur.

Find messages

Messages now has a Catalyst app, similar to the Messages app on iOS apps with many of the same features, including the new features introduced in iOS 14.

You can pin up to nine important discussions at the top of the "Messages" app. Conversations are displayed as circular images at the top of the application. The typing display lets you see what is being typed, and new messages and Tapbacks will be moved onto the pushpin.

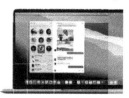

Matching answers help organize the conversation, allowing you to reply to a specific message to start a new topic that can be chosen. It's good for one-on-one conversations, but great for group conversations.

You can use pictures, memoji, or emojis to personalize group conversations, and "mentions" can direct messages to specific people. If a group conversation is muted continuously and someone is talking to you in conversation, you can ask them to send you a notification so you don't miss out on important moments in the conversation.

There's a new "image" option in the email app with Memoji plugins (can be done with Memoji editor for the first time on a Mac), to find trending images and GIFs by searching of #images, and message effects on iOS. Available for several years.

Available in message effects (such as balloons, confetti, lasers, and more.

Emails are easy to find, and search results can be organized into links, images, and keywords.

map

According to memos, Apple has improved the Mac version of Maps, taking the features that are limited to iOS, and adding the features to iOS 14.

You can plan a route with a bike path on your Mac and send it to iOS. The nature of the paths depends on the height, solid pathways, stairs, and so on. In addition, there are several options for designing access roads that include parking lots.

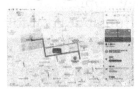

A guide created by trusted authorities and partners that lists tips for dining, shopping, and sightseeing in cities around the world. You can create your guide in macOS Big Sur's Maps app and then share it with friends and family.

macOS Big Sur adds a "look around" feature to the "Maps" app, which allows you to explore the city at high street level, as well as the maps inside, you can see in airports and shops to prepare yourself before leaving the arrangement.

The latest features of the ETA section can be found in the Map app, so you can keep track of the progress of people sharing the same ETA on the Mac. Apple-specific maps will be available in Canada, Ireland, and the United States. 2020 UK.

More features

Spotlights

Searching with Spotlight in Finder is faster than ever, and results are displayed in a simplified list, which is easier to pronounce.

With Spotlight's "Quick View" feature, you can use quick editing tools such as editing, PDF signing, and more, to create full-fledged rollbacks of your files. all documents or websites. You can use the quick review tool so you can make quick edits without having to install the software.

Now a Spotlight can load the "Find" menu in Safari, Pages, Keynote, and other applications.

Quick user interface

macOS Big Sur has an advanced conversion feature, designed to allow you to quickly and easily convert user files without having to quit and restart your Mac. It's similar to the quick conversion feature available to Windows users.

Software Store

Apple has added "label tags" to apps in the App Store and Mac App Store, which keep track of information from developers about the data collected and whether or not you use it. this information will track you across other programs and sites, so you can make informed decisions about The programs you download.

Developers need to demonstrate this knowledge to themselves. Developers who didn't get involved and gave false information that their apps would be removed from the App Store during the review may be worried.

Apple Arcade includes an in-depth Game-app interface, which lets you view your friends' favorite games, view games with achievements and highlights, and see information on play through the Game Center display.

Apple Arcade in Big Sur offers replayable games that can be found on the Apple Arcade platform, so you can easily switch between platforms. There are several new filters to access Apple Arcade data, including the Apple Arcade section of the App Store, which includes quick preview information about upcoming games.

App developers can make internal purchases and signups between family members, so more people can use the signup process.

Photograph

The "Images" application has an additional feature that can remove unwanted information from images, as well as a single all-in-one image editor for editing videos.

The vividness in the image can be adjusted, and the intensity of the filter and the light effect of the image can be adjusted for better editing.

The subtitles function allows the words in an image to be combined with another search term, called "subtitles", and then added to the new iOS "subtitles" option. 14.

AirPods

With macOS Big Sur and iOS 14, AirPods can switch between working devices on the same iCloud account.

So, if you watch a video on an iPhone and then switch to a Mac, AirPods can switch between iPhone and Mac without using a Bluetooth connection to switch between devices.

Home box

HomeKit home appliances supported by security cameras now have the full support and video experience. With the help of the eyepiece, the camera can see the person's name from the "Photos" app, so it can see friends and family who are showing you what's on. the door recorded in the video.

The worksheet will leave out some parts of the upper movement so that you can customize the movement of the movement.

The HomeKit LED flashlight can use a new adaptive lighting feature of lighting called Night Shift to change colors around the world. It will change the temperature of the electric light throughout the day and reduce the blue light at night.

The home application also provides a state-of-the-art system, allowing you to focus on important information to know and information that needs to be looked at, such as minimums and related issues. , Or to install new ones

Apple Music

"For You" on Apple Music has been replaced by "Listen Now", a platform that offers new albums, artist interviews, and personal collection lists in one place. It's similar to "Serving You", but focuses more on personal information and newly released products.

A search on Apple Music combines different genres and songs related to categories such as "Summertime Sounds", making it easier to find new songs.

Memo

As with iOS, the "Pin Style" function can be increased or dropped, and word types and custom options can be retrieved at once using the new "Quick Style" function.

You can search for "popular searches" on the most relevant topics, and the scanner is more efficient for the Continuous Web, which achieves the best scanning results by improving the search. level cutting.

Memories

Current memories can be shared with people who share the same list, and thoughts about memories you have made in the past can be shared. You can customize the list with emojis, other customization options for smart lists, better searches than ever before, and some keyboard shortcuts for navigation. List and change dates.

the sky

The "Weather" widget provides government alerts for major seasonal events, provides detailed information when major temperature changes occur, and provides detailed information about rainfall.

macOS Battery life

How to disable chart view to be installed on macOS

At macOS Big Sur, Apple has introduced a smart feature de-signed to learn from your installation method and extend bat-tery life by minimizing the time it takes for a Mac laptop to carry.

After accessing this feature (by default, on Macs with an Apple M1 chip or a T2 security chip), the Mac will try to learn the download process to ensure a full download of the Mac after extracting the power source. When normal operation is com-pleted, the Mac will delay ordering by more than 80% in some cases.

Of course, if you don't set a routine, then this routine may be problematic. For example, you may end up disconnecting your Mac and not using it for a long time, only to find that it doesn't pay enough if you want it.

Mac is fully charged If you first know you want to get your Mac up and running quickly, you can click the icon in the menu bar at any time, then select "full now" time "in the fixed site direc-tory.

However, if you need to quickly disconnect your Mac, this is not an option, it is better to completely disable "Optimize Battery Charging". The next steps will show you how to do it.

How to stop or stop the charge of good electricity

1. Click the Apple icon (☐) in the left-hand corner of the desktop menu at the top of the screen, then click "System Prefers ...".

2. Select the desired file page.

3. Select "Battery" on the right side and open the box on the next side of "Optimize battery life."

4. Choose "Close" or "Tomorrow until tomorrow".

Cell health care is another feature of the Mac that is designed to extend the life of batteries. You can learn more about storekeepers' health care in our practice guide article.

How to check the electrical health of Apple Silicon MacBook

Apple's silicone-based laptops are fully equipped with battery life, a feature designed to extend battery life and the health of the Mac by reducing the number of batteries. Old chemistry.

Mac laptops use lithium-ion batteries, such as rechargeable batteries, which decrease in quality with age, but chemical life does not depend on time. It is also influenced by factors such as the history of temperature measurement and return processes.

Therefore, a personal health professional can intelligently analyze the stability status of a Mac and its performance, and based on this knowledge, this feature can sometimes reduce the power of the most powerful device. . This will ensure that your chart is paid at a level that is prepared for your use, thereby reducing the wearer's burden and slowing down its engine age.

You can follow the simple steps below to check the hardware health of a Mac powered by an Apple device.

1. Click the Apple icon (□) in the left-hand corner of the desktop menu at the top of the screen, then click "System Prefers ...".

Conversion

2. Select the desired file page.

3. Select "Battery" on the sidebar and click the "Health Battery ..." button.

Verify the "Battery status" setting. If it is normal, the battery life is good. This may be the case if the accuracy is not 100%. This is because the battery used in a Mac notebook can retain

80% of its original capacity under most operating conditions under normal conditions.

However, if Mac's battery capacity is more than 80%, it indicates that it needs to be repaired, which significantly reduces the battery life.

Every new Mac purchased from Apple has a one-year warranty, which includes service coverage for defective budgets. If your Mac isn't covered by the warranty and the battery is old, Apple can offer battery service to charge a fee.

macOS Catalina 10.15.5 Beta also introduces battery health driver for Mac

With macOS Catalina 10.15.5, Apple introduced the Mac OS firmware to Mac for the first time and introduced this functionality on Macs with Thunderbolt 3 ports.

Apple has shared detailed information about the health care of investors with sites such as Six Colors, TechCrunch, and The Verge, giving us an idea of what to expect to release. macOS Catalina 10.15.5 is available to the public.

Electronic health care aims to extend the overall life of Mac laptops by reducing the number of chemical aging. This model will analyze the stable health of the kidney and its regenerative function. In some cases, when the MacBook is not fully charged, the battery can be stored safely, as this will shorten the battery life.

When the Mac is plugged in and the battery is fully charged most of the time, the drive health function will melt and stop charging when it is fully charged.

Apple has been using the built-in health driver function in its iPhone for many years, and when the device was first introduced, there was a lot of confusion about not knowing how to implement it.

On the iPhone, the electric charging function reduces the speed of the operator during high usage to prevent the iPhone from shutting down when the electric power is reduced. The Mac works differently, and in some cases, the full charge is limited.

Once macOS Catalina 10.15.5 is installed, health can be eliminated by checking the new "Energy Saver" option in the "Energy Saver" section of the "System Prefers" app.

The battery health driver is a new feature to the macOS Catalina 10.15.5 beta second version of the power and is limited to developers. When macOS Catalina 10.15.5 is released, it will be available to all users.

Customize your macOS

Customize your Mac with system requirements

You can change the system settings to customize your Mac. For example, you can change the size and position of the Dock, choose a light or dark view, change the desktop image, etc.

To change system preferences on your Mac, click the "System Prefers" page in the Dock, and select the "Apple"> "System Prefers" menu.

Search web preferences

Mac options are set by preference. For example, the options that can be set for Spotlight are in Spotlight preferences.

Preferences are expressed in the form of icons; the images displayed may change depending on the Mac and the applications installed. Click on an icon to open the desired page, then see the options.

Set the options to the desired response

Each desired answer has options that you can customize. Most pages click the "Help" button to find out more about these options.

Pages that want to be protected on the Mac are locked. If the lock is on the left side of the page, click to open the options page.

See options in System Options

If you do not know where to find the Web preferences option, please use the search field at the top of the window. The options that match your word are listed and the answer is where they are found.

Customize system preferences

- Hide preferences: choose "View"> "Customize", uncheck the selection boxes, and click "Create" at the top of the window.
- Show hidden preferences: choose Information> Personalization, select the checkboxes for hidden preferences, and click Finish at the top of the window.
- Sort preferences: choose View> Sort by Category or Sort Alphabetically.

If you see a red tick in the "System Prefers" icon in the Dock, you need to perform one or more actions. For example, if you don't properly configure iCloud, the icon will appear in the dock in the Dock; otherwise, the symbol will appear on the screen. When you click on the sign, favorites are displayed so that you can complete the settings.

To change the options of an application, such as Mail or Safari, open the application, click the name of the application in the main menu, and select "Preferences." None of the programs provide preferences.

Run Windows on Mac

With Boot Camp, you can install and run Windows on Intel-powered Macs.

The Boot Camp Assistant can help you set up a Windows partition on the inside of your Mac computer, and then begin installing Windows software.

After installing Windows drivers and Boot Camp, you can start your Mac on Windows or macOS.

For information about installing Windows using Boot Camp, please see Camp's help guide.

Edit the image for yourself or others in the program on your Mac

You can change the image shown to you and others in an application (for example by email or mail) on your Mac.

Tip: You can change the login image displayed on the page with your username or other usernames in the login screen on your Mac.

The picture is in the letter

Emails can include photos of you and the person who sent you the email, in conjunction with photos found in the Contact Request. The images are only shown to you; Not included in your email address. See Show photos of people in messages.

The picture is in the letter

The photos of you and your friends are shown in the message may be different.

- If you share photos or Memoji with your friends (using macOS Big Sur), they will see the photos you have shared, and you will see their photos. See how to share your name and photo in "Messages."

- If you and your friends don't share photos or Memoji (using macOS Big Sur), or your friends are using macOS 10.15 or earlier, they'll see their photos download the Contacts app, and you'll also see pictures of them in your "Contacts" app.

Picture in Contacts

You can add photos to affiliate cards and attach photos of the attachment to their affiliate card (these images can be found in other applications). Your contacts will not be able to see the image you have chosen, only you. See Adding or Editing an attachment image in Contacts.

Customize a desktop image on Mac

You can select the image displayed on the desktop. The Mac comes with several graphics to choose from, or you can use your graphics and choose a solid color.

Tip: You can drag an image from the desktop or archive to the thumbnail at the top of the answer to use the image as a desktop.

1. On a Mac, select the Apple menu> "System Prefers", click "Desktop and Screen Saver," and then click "Desktop."
2. On the left, see the image or color.
   - Share images and colors with your Mac: Click the arrow on the Apple page and select a folder, such as "Desktop Images" or "Colors" to see thumbnails of available images and colors.

The dynamic landscape around the day can only be changed according to your current location. If "Service Location" is disabled in the "Policy" options, the image will change according to the time displayed in the "Date and Time" preferences.

Some provide a vibrant background image, so the screensaver will not turn a dark or dull look. For example, if a black image is selected during macOS configuration, the desktop image will be set as a soft black image. To use or disable the use of graphics (if available), click the pop-up menu and select an option.

- Your photo: Click the flower next to the photo (or iPhoto, if available). If your photos are in "Images" or another folder, click the arrow on the "Folders" page and select a folder.

To add a folder, click the "Add" button, navigate to and select the folder, and click "Select".

If you don't see anything when you select a file in the images, they don't have the correct file — JPEG, PICT, TIFF, PNG, or HEIC. To change the look of the image, open it in Preview and save it to the new version. If the image is ambiguous, try using a larger image, such as 1024 x 768 pixels. 3. On the right, click the image you want to use.

The screen changes quickly, so you can see what the picture looks like. Using your images, you can choose to fill the screen, center them, or arrange them in other ways. You can browse around and try different images and settings until you find one that you like best.

To use all the images in the archive, select the "Edit" checkbox" and select the times you want to change the images, for example hourly. Images are displayed in the order in which they appear in the archive, or you can choose to show them a selection process.

Quickly use the images in the "Photos" application, select the image in "Images", click the "Share" button in the "Photos" tool, and then select "Set Desktop Picture".

You can use the images you see on the site as desktop images. In the window, press the Control key and click the image, then select "Use the image as desktop image".

Use features accessibility on Mac

The Mac's default configuration can be configured. If you're having trouble with vision, hearing, or physical activity, macOS also includes features to help you do other things — and it's easy for a Mac to use.

Use a built-in screen reader called VoiceOver

VoiceOver is a built-in audio reader on the Mac that can interpret aloud what is displayed on the screen and speak words to documents, web pages, and windows. With VoiceOver, you can governor your Mac with keyboard or trackpad gestures, and add a comfortable braille display for use with VoiceOver. To customize VoiceOver, use the VoiceOver Utility. See the VoiceOver User Guide.

Increase the information on the screen

- You can use the mouse or trackpad to zoom in to enlarge the screen or a portion of it. If you want to use a second display on your Mac, you can select the display you want to expand, or you can combine two displays at the same time.
- You can use "Hover Text" to zoom out of everything under the pointer (words, fields, placeholders, buttons, etc.) in a separate window. with high resolutions.

Decrease the movement on the chart

If you have trouble with movement on the Mac screen, you can set an option to reduce movement when using certain functions (such as Spaces, Notification Center, or Dock).

Use the keyboard shortcut or the keyboard shortcut

You can set the options to be "Sticky Keys" and "Slow Keys" to make it easier to press keys on the keyboard. Alternatively, you can remove the body image and use the screen that can be drawn on the screen.

Use tactics to control the movement and movement of the mouse

- When mouse buttons are available, you can use the keyboard or keyboard to control the direction.
- When instructional activities are available, you can use short notes, helpful hints, or facial expressions (such as smiling or opening your mouth) to create a mouse action (e.g., left-click and drag-and-drop operations).
- After the head pointer is reached, you can move the pointer based on the movement of the face or the head as seen by Mac's built-in or attached camera.

Use voice control and speech recognition

- With voice management, you can use voice commands on your Mac to open programs, select hard drive directories, and more. macOS offers a set of standard commands, you can create your commands. See Use voice control to control your Mac and apps.
- You can speak to your Mac in conversations and notifications, and alert you when the app requires you to perform certain actions (such as accepting a message invitation). Notice that the Mac speaks the word on the chart.

Change the way the keyboard, mouse, and trackpad work

- You can set various options to customize how the keyboard, mouse, and trackpad work when using a Mac. For example, when you move your finger on the trackpad, you can adjust the speed at which the direction moves on the chart. To set these options, select the

Apple menu> "System Prefers" and click "Keyboard", "Mouse" or "Trackpad".

Use the helpful tools to control your Mac

- With the Switch Switch, you can use one or more connectors to enter text, interact with objects on the screen, and control your Mac. The switch controls the panel or user interface until the switch is used to select an object and perform an action. Look at the switch usage.
- Using a user-friendly keyboard, you can use Sit with a touch screen to make it easier to enter text, interact with objects on the chart, and control on the Mac. Using the chair, you can sit on the couch for a specific time to perform mouse actions. Learn how to use the residential directions.

You can use the Shortcut panel to enable or disable any feature in the image.

Use your web account on a Mac

By connecting the database to Mac, Exchange, Google, Yahoo, and other web accounts it can be used in Mac applications.

You can connect Internet accounts and manage account settings in the "Internet Services" options. You can connect web accounts from some programs that use web accounts.

iCloud archives are displayed using the iCloud options in the Apple ID preferences that are displayed in the "Internet Explorer" preferences. You can change its setting everywhere.

Add the number through the program

You can add accounts from "Letters", "Associates" and "Calendar". The file you added from the application will be displayed in the "Internet Explorer" options.

1. To apply on your Mac, click the application menu and select "Add Account".
For example, in "Mail", select "Mail"> "Add Account".
2. Select your account provider and follow the instructions on the chart.

If you would like to add an account from an unlisted provider, such as a business or email or calendar account, click "Other [Account Information]", click "Continue", and enter the account setting required. If you are unsure of financial accounting settings, please consult your lender.

Add an account in the "Web Hosting" options

Before you can add an account in the preferences of the Website, you must create an archive on the provider's website.

Note: If you want to set up and use iCloud for the first time, please refer to setting up an Apple ID.

1. On a Mac, select the Apple menu> "System Prefers" and click "System Prefers."
2. Click on a donor.

If you don't have an account from a specific source (such as Yahoo), create an account on that provider's website and link it here.

If you would like to add an account for an unlisted provider, such as an email or calendar account for a business or school, click "Add another account" on the right, click the type of account you want to connect to, and enter the account for which the settings are requested. If you do not know the type of account or financial settings, please ask your lender.

3. Enter your account username, password, and required information.

4. If the task list contains the number attached to the right, select the task you want to use.

Change financial accounting features and details

1. On a Mac, select the Apple menu> "System Prefers" and click "System Prefers."
2. Select the file on the left, and then do one of the following:

   • Turn on or off features: select each feature you want to use, then select the features you don't want to use.
   • Edit account information: For the selected account, click "Information" on the right. Some accounts display the account name, description, and other details on the right side, without the "detail" button.

Prevent account usage

1. On a Mac, select the Apple menu> "System Prefers" and click "System Prefers."
2. Select the file you want to stop using, and then do one of the following:
   • Delete an account and finish its operation: press the delete button.

If your Mac is set up to use iCloud Keychain and you delete an account (not a large iCloud account), you will be prompted to delete that account from other Mac computers set up for iCloud Keychain or close to all the numbers are features on this Mac.
   • Finish a specific task: remove it.

Example: Deleting an account or turning off each feature will delete the data stored in your application. If you search for this feature and reconnect the account, the data may be restored. If you are unsure, please ask your lender.

Manage users, guests, and groups on Mac

If your Mac has multiple users, you'll need to set up an account for each person so that everyone can customize the settings and options without anyone else. You can allow occasional users to log in as guests without having to download files or the settings of other users. You can create groups. You need an administrator on your Mac to perform these tasks.

The user and organization preferences indicate the selected user in the user list. The "Password" page, the "Login Item" page, and the "Change Password" button on the right.

Add the user

1. On a Mac, select the Apple menu> "System Prefers" and then click "Users and organizations."

If the lock is on the left side, click on it to open the desired side.

2. tap the Add switch below the user list.
3. Click the "New Website" pop-up menu and select a user.
   - Administrator: The administrator can connect and manage other users, upload requests, and change settings. The new user created when Mac was first configured was the administrator. Your Mac can have multiple administrators. You can create new users and change regular users to administrators. Do not set up a login for administrators. If you do, someone can restart the Mac and get access with administrator privileges. To ensure the security of your Mac, please do not share the administrator's username and password.
   - Default: Standard users are set by the administrator. Ordinary users can install programs and change their settings, but cannot connect to other users or change the settings of other users.
   - Sharing: Sharing users can remotely download shared files, but cannot access or change settings

on the computer. To allow users to access isolated or protected files, you may need to change the settings in the "File Sharing", "Sharing Sharing" or "Remote Management" sections of "Sharing" preferences. See Set up file sharing and share on the screen of another Mac.

To learn more about the options for each user, click the "Help" button on the left-hand side of the dialog box.

4. Enter the full name of the new user. Account name created. Use an unalike account name, enter it now-you can't change it later.

5. Enter the user's password, then re-enter it for verification. Enter a password to help users remember the password.

6. Click User Action.

7. Depending on the type of user you create, you can do any of the following:
   - For administrators, choose "Permit users to sail across this computer."
   - For the administrator, choose "Allow users to reset their keywords using Apple ID".
   - Use share preferences to determine if users can share your file and share screens.

For information about Apple's privacy policy, please visit Apple's Privacy Policy website.

If your Mac has a Touch ID, new users can connect fingerprints after logging in to the Mac. Users can use Touch ID to unlock Macs and password-protected devices and use their Apple ID to purchase items from the iTunes Store, App Store, and Apple Books. Learn how to use a touch ID.

Create a team

Companies allow multiple users to share the same responsibility. For example, you can assign groups access rights to files or files, and group members have all rights. You can grant specific permissions to each shared file.

The preferences of the user and the group are displayed to the left of the selected group; the names of the organization and members are displayed on the right.

1. On a Mac, select the Apple menu> "System Prefers" and then click "Users and organizations."

If the lock is on the left side, click on it to open the desired side.

2. Tap the Add switch below the user list.
3. tap the "New Website" pop-up menu and choose "Group".
4. Give the group a name and click Create Group.
5. Select each user and group that you want to add to the new group.

Use the sharing options to specify whether members of the group can share files and share screens.

Convert users usually to managers

1. On a Mac, select the Apple menu> "System Prefers" and then click "Users and organizations."

If the lock is on the left side, click on it to open the desired side.

2. Select a custom user or admin user in the user list, and then select "Allow user to navigate this computer".

Allow users at any time as guests

You can allow other people to use the Mac as a guest user without having to connect to it as a user.

- Visitors can log in without a password.
- Visitors cannot change user or computer settings.
- After turning on remote access in the "Sharing" options, visitors will not be able to access remotely.

Files created by the guest are stored in a repository, but when the guest leaves, the repository, and its contents are deleted.

Guest login is used with the "Find Me" request to help you find your Mac if it's lost. If someone sees your Mac, you can find it, log in as a guest, and then use Safari to access the site. Please click the "Find my apps" settings to see which Mac is missing.

Note: If FileVault is turned on, visitors can visit Safari, but will not be able to download your encrypted code and create files.

1. On a Mac, select the Apple menu> "System Prefers" and then click "Users and organizations."

If the lock is on the left side, click on it to open the desired side.

2. Select "Guest user" in the user list.
3. Select "Allow visitors to access this computer."
4. If you prefer, please select "Block adult sites" to prevent visitors from accessing adult sites.
5. To allow visitors to use shared files on another computer on the site, select "Allow guest users to add shared files."

Privacy of access information

If you are an administrator, you can direct the window view to all other users.

1. On a Mac, select the Apple menu> "System Prefers", click "Users and Groups", and then click "Your Accessibility Options."

If the lock is on the left side, click on it to open the desired side.

2. Click the "Auto Login" pop-up menu, then select a user, and select "Close".

If you select a user, the user will only leave when the Mac starts. If you select "Off", the Mac will open a window to show all users when it starts. The automatic login will clear the next time you restart your Mac.

Note: Allow someone to access your Mac by restarting the Mac. If you can access it, make sure your Mac is not locked to the administrator. When FileVault is converted, automatic access will not stop.

    3. choose the desired option. If you have any requests, please tap the "Help" button for more information.

To allow new users to access your shared or protected file, you must change the settings for file sharing, shared protection, or remote response. of the Proclamation Concept. See Set up file sharing and share on the screen of another Mac.

Open the "Sharing" options, select the "Apple" menu> "System Prefers" and click "Sharing."

Make it easy for you to view information on the Mac screen

If you're having trouble seeing what's on the screen when you're using a Mac, please try other ideas.

Change the appearance of the desktop

- To reduce desktop transparency: select the Apple menu> "System Prefers", click "Accessibility", click "Display", then click "Display", then select "Reduce Transparency". The glass pieces on the desk and the application glass windows are gray.
- Select a desktop image with colors and small shapes: select the menu "Apple"> "System Prefers", click "Desktop and Screen Saver", click "Desktop", view the image library to the left, and the right, select images or non-permanent colors.
- To darken the border: select the Apple menu> "System Prefers", click "Accessibility", click "Display", then click "Display", then select "Increase Contrast". macOS will reduce transparency and make the borders of buttons, boxes, etc. on the chart more visible.
- To use a dark appearance: select the Apple menu>

"System Prefers", click "General", and then click "Dark Appearance". You can change the look and apply the color.

- Find the color: select the "Apple"> "System Prefers" menu, click "Accessibility", "Display", "Display", and then select "Invert Color". If the night conversion function is enabled, the "different color conversion" will not disappear.
- Lighten the eyes with color at night: Use the Night Shift to warm the colors on the screen.
- Separate or subtract color: apply color filters and color the entire layer.
- To add direction: select the Apple menu> "System Prefers", click "Accessibility", click "Display", click "Cursor", then drag the "Cursor Size" slide to the right and the desired size.

Hint: If you can't control the direction on the chart, quickly move your finger on the trackpad or move quickly with the mouse — the pointer will be too short for you to see. To end this feature, select the Apple menu> "System Prefers", click "Accessibility", "Display", "Cursor", and then deselect the "Shake the mouse point to find" option.

Make text bigger

- Increase the number of emails to "Mail": in "Mail", select "Mail"> "Prefers", click "Font and Color", click "Select" on the "Mail Font" page, then click Select Font Size in the Font window.
- Increase the digit of messages in "Messages": in "Messages", choose "Messages"> "Preferences", click "General", and then move to the "Size" slide. text "to the right.
- Increase the amount of language in other applications: In most applications, you can press Command-Plus (+) or Command-Minus (-) to adjust the amount of lan-

guage. If this does not work, check the requirements of the application.

Make icons and other items bigger

- Increase the size of icons and text on the desktop: hold down the Control key and click on the screen, select "Show View Option", then move the "Icon Size" slide to the right Click in the "Text Size" pop-up menu and select a word size.
- Increase the number of icons and words in the Finder: Select an item in the Finder, and then select Information> Display Options. The information you use will determine the size.
  - Sign view: Move the "Large Sign" slider to the right. tap the "Text Size" pop-up menu and select a word size.
  - List view: select the icon size to the right of "Icon size". Click the "Text Size" pop-up menu and select a word size.
  - View Columns: Click the "Text Size" pop-up menu, then select a word size. You cannot select the size of the icon.
  - View Gallery: select the smallest size. You cannot specify the amount of language.
- Increase the size of items in the Finder and Mail sidebars: select the Apple menu> "System Prefers", click "General", click the "Sidebar Icon Size" pop-up menu, and then the main course".

Use approximation

- Zoom in on the screen: select the menu "Apple"> "Your Default Settings", click "Accessibility", and then click "Zoom." You can attach the entire screen or part of the screen.
  - After selecting "Use shortcuts to zoom in", you can zoom in (click the Option-Command-like sign),

zoom out (click the Option-Command-minus sign), or change quickly. between the two settings (click Option-Command- 8).

- When "Use scroll movements with zoom switches" is selected, you can click by holding down the Control key (or a shift key) and jump up on the trackpad with two fingers.

· Navigate to the items under the menu: select the Apple menu> "Prefers System ", click" Accessibility ", click" Zoom ", then select" Enable hover text. "Study how to use the word, however.

· Zoom in on a site: In Safari, select View> Zoom In, or press Command-Plus (+). You can select "zoom" and press Command-Plus several times to continue zooming. If you want to scale the text instead of the images, select "Scale Text Only".

· Increase PDFs, images, and web pages: If your mouse or trackpad supports it, you can use pretentious systems to zoom in or out. Select the "Apple" menu> "System Prefers", click "Mouse"> "Zoom and click" or "Trackpad"> "Zoom and zoom", and then select "Smart Zoom". Now to zoom in or out, use one finger to double-click on the mouse, or use two fingers to double-click on the touchpad.

Use a firewall on your Mac

When you're away from your Mac or want more privacy, you can use a firewall to hide the desktop.

1. On a Mac, select the Apple menu> "System Prefers", click "Desktop and Screen Saver", and then click "Screen

Saver".

2. Click the screen saver on the left, then set the options for its appearance on the right.

The available options vary depending on the screen saver you select.

- Source: Click the pop-up menu, then select the image you want to display on the screen. You can use macOS -linked images, or you can select images from the image library or other libraries.

The preview area shows the appearance of the guard. Give him or her a moment to review your options.

- Arrange the order of the display: Select this specific box to display the images in a balanced order instead of displaying the images in order of origin.
- Protective protection options: Click to set options such as color, speed, and so on.

3. Select to set the time to display the screen saver.
- Start next time: click the pop-up menu, then choose how long you want your Mac to wait before starting the backup.
- Display with clock: Select this checkbox to display the time on the screen.
- Use a single firewall: check this box to allow macOS to choose which firewall to use.
- Hotspot: Click to set a shortcut to immediately start the hotspot when needed.

Remove the screen investor and return to the desktop, press any key, move the mouse or touch the trackpad.

If you want to increase security when you stand on the security guard, see the question for a password after waking up your Mac.

Set up the protection time for yourself on the Mac

On a Mac, turn on "Time Management" to learn how to spend time on Mac and other devices. When "Time Control" is enabled, you will be able to see information showing how the application is used, the number of notifications received, and when the app is used.

The "Time Table" is the question to the "Time Table" response. Select the "Share on devices" option.

1. On a Mac, select the Apple menu> "System Prefers" and click "Time Control."
2. If you are a member of the grouped family, click on the pop-up menu on the right side of the page and select yourself.

If you are not using family sharing, there will be no pop-up menu on the page.

3. Click "Options" on the left-hand side of the page.
4. Click "Open" in the upper right corner.
5. Choose one of the following options:
   - Sharing devices: select this option if you want the "Screen Sharing" display to match the time spent on other devices logged in with the same Apple ID.

   This option is available only if you log in with your Apple ID.

   - Use a protected time password: select this option to override the protection time settings and require a password to be allowed when the time limit expires.
6. If required, do any of the following:
   - Click "Downtime" on the sidebar, and then set the time menu.
   - Click "Application Limits" on the page, and then set time limits for applications and sites.
   - Click on the conversation on the page, then set the

> conversation tabs.
> - Click "Yes" on the page and select the programs that you can use from time to time.
> - Click on "information and privacy" on the page, then set the data and privacy restrictions.

Change the language used by your Mac

Although Mac is set to display the language of the country or country of purchase, you can choose another language to use. For example, if you buy a Mac in the United States but speak fluently in French, you can configure the Mac to use French.

You can choose different languages for each request. For illustration, if your system is set to Pretentious Chinese, but you want an application in English, you can do so.

Change the language system

1. On a Mac, select the Apple menu> "System Prefers" and then click "Language and Country."
2. Click General.
3. Do any of the following:
   - Add words: Click the Add button, select one or more words from the list, and then click Add.

   The list is separated by a separate line. The on -line language is the operating language fully supported by macOS and is displayed in menus, messages, settings, etc. macOS does not fully support the languages below this line, but any of the programs you use can mature these words, and these requests are displayed in menus and messages and on certain websites.

   If you are unable to use the input source selected in the input directory to type the selected language, a list of available resources will be displayed. If you do not currently add an input resource, you can add it later in the Source menu of Keyboard preferences.

- Change language: select another language from the language list.

If macOS or the application supports a major language, menus and messages will be displayed in that language. If not, it will use the language not selected in the list, and so on. This language can also be used on websites that support this language.

The order of the words in the list determines how the meaning of the word is determined when you type the words in the text that are related to the same language. Check if non -Latin characters are not displayed correctly on the Mac.

If you have a lot of Mac users and you want everyone to see the first language you chose in the login window, click the "Tasks" pop-up menu and select "Ask Window Window "

Select the language to use for each application

1. On a Mac, select the Apple menu> "System Prefers" and then click "Language and Country."
2. Click on the application.
3. Do any of the following:
   - Select a language for the application: click the Add button, select the application and language from the pop-up menu, and click Add.
   - Change the language of the application in the list: select the application, then choose a new language from the pop-up menu.
   - Remove an application from the list: select the application, and then click the "Remove" button. The program reuses the default language.

If the program is uninstalled, you may need to close and re-open it to see the changes.

Basics

Use the help in Mac

The one available and most applications on the Mac have a "Help" menu in the base menu, so you can easily get information about macOS, Mac, and the programs you use.

Tip: If you see a "Help" button in the user's experience (for example, on the options page or dialog box), click the button to get options related to the answer. or the dialog box you see in Table A and the activity description.

Use the help menu

In the application in the Finder or Mac, select "Help" in the hard drive menu, and then do any of the following.

- Open the macOS user guide or the user guide of an application: select macOS help or [Help] help (e.g. email help).
- Search for products or resources: Start by typing a word into the search field. The "Help" directory lists directory products and helps with current related topics.

To find where the menu item is, move the cursor over the menu item. To open a help topic in the help window, select it in the list. Or select "Show all help topics".

Use the help glass window

Whether you use the macOS user guide or the user guide for the program, you can easily browse additional topics, search for guides, etc.

In the user guide on a Mac, do any of the following:

- Find Help Tips: Enter a word in the search field, then select Help Suggestions or click Return.
- Show or hide more topics: Click the "Directory" button.
- Indicates the first topic or topic you are looking at: click the front and back buttons.
- View a list of revised topics: Click and hold the "Back" or "Forward" button until the list is listed, then select the desired topic.
- Increase or decrease the wording: Press Command-Plus (+) or Command-Minus (-).
- Add more glass: drag the right side or bottom of the glass.
- Find a word in the present topic: Press-F, and then enter the word you want to find.
- Click or share a topic: Click the "Share" button in the help window, then select an option.

If you are unable to find what you are looking for while searching for help, please try entering another word or fewer words in the search engine. help box.

Increase or decrease Mac volume

To change the volume on a Mac, click the "Volume" button on the menu bar, then drag the slider to adjust the volume (or use the navigation bar).

If there is no "Volume" control in the menu bar, select the "Apple" menu> "System Prefers", then click "Sound". Check the "Show volume in menu bar" checkbox.

Connect your Mac to the internet

Now, whether you're at home, in the office, or on the go, you can easily connect to the Web from your Mac. There are two main ways to surf the Internet using Wi-Fi (wireless) or Ethernet (wired) connections. If you don't have one, you can use a hotspot.

Use Wi-Fi

When the Mac can use the Wi-Fi network, the Wi-Fi icon will appear in the desktop menu at the top of the screen. Click the icon, and then select a site to join. If you see a lock on the side of the network name, it means that the network is protected by a password - you must enter the password before you can use the Wi-Fi network. How to connect using Wi-Fi.

Use Ethernet

You can use Ethernet over Ethernet or DSL or a cable modem. If Ethernet is available, connect the Ethernet cable to the Ethernet port on the Mac (indicated by this symbol). If you don't have Ethernet Ethernet built into your Mac, you can use an adapter to connect the Ethernet cable to a USB or Thunderbolt port on your computer. How to use an Ethernet connection.

Use the hotspot

If you can't access Wi-Fi or Ethernet networks, you can use a Mac and Instant Hotspot to bond to the Internet via a personal link on your iPhone or iPad. How to attach using iPhone or iPad.

At home, work at, or on the go

When you live at home: your ISP may provide a Wi-Fi or Ethernet connection. In case you do not know how to log in, please call your ISP.

Hours: You have a Wi-Fi or Ethernet connection. Please contact your IT professional or system administrator for detailed information about installing your operating system and user policies.

On the go: You can use Wi-Fi hotspots (a wireless network open to the public) on your Mac or Instant Hotspot on your Mac (if supported by your Mac or device) phone) Please note that some Wi-Fi hotspots require you to enter a password, agree to the terms of service or pay for use.

Use macOS shortcuts

You can use key combinations called keyboard shortcuts to speed up tasks on your Mac. Keyboard shortcuts include one or more switch keys (such as Caps Lock or Control) and the back key. Press these keys at the same time. For example, instead of moving the cursor on the menu bar to select File> New Window, you can press the Command and N keys.

You can change or delete keyboard shortcuts to make them easier to use.

Find macOS shortcuts

Briefs are displayed on the instructions page in the macOS application. Many keyboard shortcuts are common functions in the application.

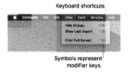

Guides to many macOS programs contain a list of shortcuts that are often used for the application. For example, see:

- Shortcuts of the Safari tour
- Short email address
- Short photo clips and symbols
- Short disk drive
- Short preview

Tip: You can find shortcuts on the Apple support page for Mac keyboard shortcuts.

Use shortcuts to perform tasks

- Hold down one or more switch keys (such as Caps Lock, Command, or Control), and then press the last key of the shortcut.

For example, use the Command-V keyboard shortcut to paste the copied letters, press and hold the Command key at the same time as the V key, and then release both keys.

Customize short stories

You can customize some keyboard shortcuts by changing the key combination.

1. On a Mac, select the Apple menu> "System Prefers", click "Keyboard", and then click "Shortcuts."
2. In the menu on the left, select a category, such as "Mission Control" or "Spotlight."
3. In the list on the right, select the checkbox after the shortcut you want to change.
4. Double-click the current key combination, and then click the new key combination you want to use.

You cannot use each key (for example, letter keys) multiple times in a key combination.

5. Exit and re-open all the applications you are using to perform the new keyboard shortcuts.

If you provide a shortcut that stands for another command or request, the new key path will not be received. Find the keyboard command you are using, and then provide another keyboard shortcut for that item.

If you want to bring back all shortcuts to the keyboard combination, go to the "Shortcuts" page of the "Keyboard" preferences and click "Restore Defaults."

Disable keyboard shortcuts

Sometimes, the shortcuts of an application conflict with macOS shortcuts. If this is the case, you can disable macOS keyboard shortcuts.

1. On a Mac, select the Apple menu> "System Prefers", click "Keyboard", and then click "Shortcuts."
2. In the menu on the left, select a category, such as "Mission Control" or "Spotlight."
3. In the list on the right, open the option on the page on the short page you want to finish.

Go online with Safari on Mac

Using Safari, you can easily navigate to the website you want.

Go online

1. In the Safari app on the Mac, enter the name or URL of the page in the "Smart Search" field.

As you type, Safari tips will be displayed.

2. Select an idea, and press Enter to go directly to the address you entered.

See Use Safari find what you want.

See the link to the website

1. In the Safari app on the Mac, navigate to the navigation above the link.
2. Make sure the network interface is at the default level at the bottom of the window.
   - If you do not see the status, select Information> Limit Display.
   - If the trackpad supports it, it should click on the link to preview the information.

Change the brightness of the Mac display

You can adjust the brightness of the look manually or without.

Use the glittering key

If the color is too dark, you can adjust the brightness.

- On a Mac, press the brightness increase key or the brightness decrease key (or use the navigation bar).

Properly adjust the brightness

1. If your Mac has a flashlight, select the "Apple" menu> "System Prefers", click "Displays", and then click "Displays".
2. Select "Configure Settings".

If you don't see the "Auto -adjust brightness" checkbox, you can adjust the brightness.

Hand adjust the glitter

1. On a Mac, select the Apple menu> "System Prefers", click "Display", and then click "Display".
2. Drag the "Brightness" slide adjust the brightness of the display.

Depending on the type of view associated with your Mac, you may notice a "Contrast" slider, which can be used to adjust the contrast of the monitor.

You can't control the brightness of some Apple features. In OS X 10.10 and later, the "Brightness" slide is no longer displayed in the "Display" response of the "Display" preferences.

For details on the show's brilliance, see the documentation that came with the show.

Connect a printer on Mac

To use a printer, you must add to the print list using the "Printers and Scanners" options. (If you're switching from a computer running Windows to a Mac running Mac, use the same "Printers and Scanners" requirements as using the "control" panel in Windows.)

In most cases, connecting a printer, macOS will use AirPrint to connect to the printer or simply download the printer's software (also called a printer driver). Do not install the software that came with the printer or the software on the manufacturer's website

If your printer supports AirPrint, it works with macOS. If your printer does not have AirPrint enabled, you can verify that it is compatible with macOS by visiting Apple's support article "Printer and Scanner Drivers for Mac".

To learn how to use the printer on an iPhone or iPad, see printing from an iPhone, iPad, or iPod touch using AirPrint.

Connect a USB flash drive

For most USB printers, all you need to do is upgrading the software and then bond the printer to the Mac. The only macOS will detect the printer and download the necessary software. For other printers, you may need to complete a few steps to add a print.

1. On a Mac, update the app: select the Apple menu> "System Prefers", click "System Preferences", and install all the listed app reviews. While no updates are known, this confirms macOS the latest information about the printing software that can be downloaded from Apple. If you do not do this, when you connect the printer, you may see a message stating that the software is not available.

2. Prepare the printer: Follow the instructions that came with the printer to remove the printer, apply ink or toner, and then add paper. Turn on the printer and make sure no defects are shown.
3. Connect the printer: connect the USB cable to the Mac. If you see a message warning you to download new software, make sure to download and install it.

Important: If your Mac has a single USB-C port, use a multiport adapter. Connect the printer, then connect the USB-C cable to the power supply to extend the life of your Mac tablet. Learn more about USB-C.

To learn how to use a USB to connect a printer that supports Air-Print, see how to connect a printer using other settings.

Connect to Wi-Fi or a wireless printer

If the Mac and printer are connected to the same Wi-Fi network, you can use the printer without any settings. To view, select "File"> "Print", click the "Printers" pop-up menu, select the "Nearby Printers" or "Printers and Scanners" options and select your machine. click. If you do not have a printer, you can connect one.

1. On a Mac, update the app (if you don't have an AirPrint printer): select the Apple menu> "System Prefers", click "Software Preferences", and install the listed software updates. While no updates are known, this confirms macOS the latest information about the printing software that can be downloaded from Apple. If you do not do this, when you connect the printer, you may see a message stating that the software is not available.

If you have an AirPrint printer, you don't need to check for software bring up to date.

2. Prepare the printer: Follow the instructions that came with the printer to remove the printer, apply ink or

toner, and then add paper. Turn on the printer and make sure no defects are shown.

3. Connect the printer: Follow the instructions that came with the printer to connect it to the system.

If you have a Wi-Fi printer, you will need to connect the printer to your Mac with a USB cable to set up a Wi-Fi printer. After connecting the printer to the Mac, please install the Mac software that came with the printer, and then use the printer's configuration manager to connect the printer to the Wi-Fi network. After the setup is complete, you can disconnect the cable from the printer and Mac, and the printer will always be connected to the Wi-Fi network. Please see Apple's support article on connecting AirPrint printers to Wi-Fi networks.

4. Add the printer to the list of available printers: select the Apple menu> "System Prefers", then click "Printers & Scanners".

If you do not see the printer on the left, click the "Add" button below the list. A dialog box is displayed, listing the publishers on your local site. It will take a minute or two for your printer to come out. Select the printer shown in the list, and then click Add. If you see a message prompting you to transfer new software, make sure to transfer and install it.

If your printer does not appear on the list, try to connect the printer by its IP address (see below).

Connecting to a printer, macOS can often determine if the printer is properly equipped with special features, such as new paper plates, memory cards, or a two-page printer. If this is not possible, a dialog box will be displayed that will allow you to point to the hem. Be sure to check the settings in this discussion to make sure the features of the printer are set up so that you can use them effectively.

Associate the printer by IP address

If the web printer you want to use does not have a list of available printers, you can connect it as an IP printer. The printer must support one of the other printing methods: AirPrint, HP Jetdirect (basic), Line Printer Daemon (LPD), or Internet Protocol Protocol (IPP).

Note: Some printers are about to use these standard combinations to provide borderline operations.

You need to know the IP address or hostname of the network printer, the printing protocol, and the model or printer name. If it uses a special line, you need to know the line name. Ask the person who runs the printer or server for help.

1. On a Mac, update the app (if you don't have an AirPrint printer): select the Apple menu> "System Prefers", click "Software Preferences", and install the listed software updates. While no updates are known, this confirms macOS the latest information about the printing software that can be downloaded from Apple. If you do not do this, when you connect the printer, you may see a message stating that the software is not available.

If you have an AirPrint printer, you don't need to check for software bring up to date.

2. Prepare the printer: Follow the instructions that came with the printer to remove the printer, apply ink or toner, and then add paper. Check the printer and make sure it shows no defects.

3. Connect the printer: Follow the instructions that came with the printer to connect it to the system.

See Apple's support article on connecting AirPrint printers to Wi-Fi networks.

4. Add the printer to the list of available printers: select the Apple menu> "System Prefers", then click "Printers & Scanners".

Click the Add button at the bottom of the print bar, click the IP button, and then use the next tab as a guide to enter print information.

Address

Enter the IP address of the printer (a number such as 192.168.20.11) or hostname (e.g. printer.example.com).

Protocol

Click the "Protocol" pop-up menu, then select the printer-supported option.

- AirPrint: The AirPrint protocol provides Wi-Fi, USB, and Ethernet to capture the printing and scanning options of the printer (if the specific printer supports these features). You do not need to download and install the printer to use the printer to support AirPrint. Printers such as Aurora, Brother, Canon, Dell, Epson, Fuji, Hewlett Packard, Samsung, and Xerox support the AirPrint protocol.
- HP Jetdirect-Slot: Hewlett Packard and other printer manufacturers use this slot.
- Line Printer Daemon-LPD: Older printers and printers may use this process.
- Web-Based Publishing-IPP: Current printers and printers manage this framework.

Queue

If your printer is required, enter the printer's name. If you do not know the name of the line, try leaving a blank or call your administrator.

Name

Enter a descriptive name for the printer (e.g., a color printer) so that it can be seen in the "Printer" pop-up menu.

Place

Enter a location of the printer (e.g., "outside my office") that can be found in the "Printers" pop-up menu.

Use

If this pop-up directory does not show the appropriate software for the printer, please select "Choose software. printer ", then select your printer in the" Printer Software "menu.

If your printer is not listed, try downloading and installing the printer software (called a printer) from the printer. You can try to select Universal Printer Programs from the pop-up menu.

Connect a Bluetooth printer

If your Mac is unarmed with Bluetooth, or you're using a Bluetooth Bluetooth converter, you can print without a Bluetooth - enabled printer.

1. On a Mac, update the software: select the Apple menu> "System Prefers", click "Software Settings", and install the listed software updates. While no updates are known, this confirms macOS the latest information about the printing software that can be downloaded from Apple. If you do not do this, when you connect the printer, you may see a message stating that the software is not available.

   If you have an AirPrint printer, you don't want to check for software bring up to date.

2. Prepare the printer: Follow the instructions that came with the printer to remove the printer, apply ink or toner, and then add paper. Turn on the printer and make sure no defects are shown.

3. Connect to the printer: Follow the instructions that came with the printer to make sure you are ready to connect with Bluetooth.

4. Add a Bluetooth printer to the print menu: select the Apple menu> "System Prefers", then click "Printers and Scanners". Click the Add button, and then click the Default button.

5. Select the printer on the printout menu, and then click Add. If the printer you want to see is not in the list, enter its name on the search page and press Enter.

If your printer is not listed, please make sure you have the latest Bluetooth printer installed. Please call the manufacturer to get the latest driver.

After plugging in the printer, if you see a message warning you to download new software, make sure to download and install it.

Connect a Wi-Fi or a mobile printer that needs to be configured with data

Some publishers may require you to upload a configuration file so that the printer can be viewed online with AirPrint. If you provide a configuration file to upload, please download and copy the print configuration file to your Mac, then install it.

1. On a Mac, double-click the configuration file to open it.

2. When you see a message asking if you want to include the configuration file, click Continue.
3. When you see a message asking you to confirm that you want to install the configuration file, click Install.

The information is included in the "Profiles" answer of "System Prefers". Then you can add the printer to the print list.

4. To add a printer to the printer board, select the Apple menu> "System Prefers", then click "Printers and Scanners".
5. To add a printer to the printer board, select the Apple menu> "System Prefers", then click "Printers and Scanners". Click the Add button, and then click the Default button.

6. Select the printer (listed as an AirPrint profile) in the "Printers" menu and click "Add".

If your printer is not listed, please make sure you have configured the reprint configuration file and have a web path from the computer to the printer. Please contact your administrator to obtain a new configuration file.

Take screenshots or video clips on Mac

You can use screenshots or keyboard shortcuts to take pictures (called screenshots) or video clips on your Mac. Screenshots provide a range of tools that allow you to easily take screenshots and audio recordings and provide options to control what is captured, for example, you can set a time delay and enter instructions or click.

Use screenshots to take pictures or video clips

1. On a Mac, press Shift-Command-5 (or use Launchpad)

to open the screenshot and display the tools.

2. Click on a tool to select the items you want to capture and save (or use the bar).

For a piece of screen, drag the frame to rearrange it, or drag the edge to adjust the amount of space to be captured or retained.

Action	Tool
Grab the entire shield	
Capture window	
Grab a piece of the shield	
Secure the entire shield	
Secure a piece of fabric	

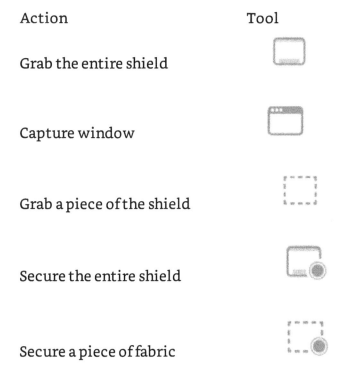

3. If necessary, click Options.

The available options change depending on whether you want to take a screenshot or a screenshot. For example, you can choose to set a timeout and display the mouse pointer or click and specify where to save the file.
The "Show Floating Thumbnails" option can help you complete a full shot or capture by easily hovering over the bot-

tom right corner of the screen for a few seconds, so you have time to drag it into the document, label it, and share it Before saving it where you point.

    4. Start a photoshoot or recording:

- For the entire screen or part of the screen: click Capture.
- For windows: move the bar to the window, then click the window.
- To record: click Record. To discontinue the recording, click the Record button in the hard drive directory.

After setting the "Show Floating Thumbnails" option, you can perform any of the other actions as the thumbnails are displayed on the bottom right of the screen.

- Swipe right to quickly save the file and disappear.
- Drag the thumbnail to a document, email, message, or Finder window.
- Click on the thumbnail to open a window where you can view the screenshot or cut the audio recording or share it.

Deployed where you choose to save the screenshot or record audio, or open an application.

Use shortcuts to take pictures

You can use a variety of shortcuts to capture images of the chart on your Mac. The file will be protected on the desktop.

Tip: To copy a screenshot so that you can paste it somewhere (such as in an email or another device), press the Control key while holding down the keys. another key. For example, to copy the entire screen, click Shift-Command-Control-3.

Action

Shortcut

Grab the entire shield

Press Shift-Command-3.

Grab a piece of the shield

Press Shift-Command-4, and then move the crosshair heading to where you want the screenshot to start. Click the mouse or trackpad button, drag where you want to capture, and then release the button or trackpad button.

Grab a window or menu bar

Press Shift-Command-4, and then press the set bar. Move the photo box pointer over the window or the hard drive menu to highlight it, then click it.

Grab menus and products directory

Open the menu, press Shift-Command-4, and then drag the command to the menu page you want to capture.

Remove the screenshot

Press Shift-Command 5.

Grab the touch yoke

Press Shift-Command-6.

You can customize these shortcuts on the "Shortcuts" page of the "Keyboard" options. On a Mac, select the Apple menu> "System Prefers", click "Keyboard", and then click "Shortcuts."

The image is saved as a .png file, and the audio recording is saved as a .mov file. The filename starts with "screenshot" or "screenshot" and is followed by a date and time.

In some applications (such as DVD Player), you may not be able to take a picture of the window.

Use Quick View to view and edit files on Mac

Quick Find gives you quick previews of all file types without having to open the file. You can share photos, cut audio and video files, and directly use "tags" in the "Quick View" window.

Tip: Use the quick find tool in the "Finder" window, desktop, email and mailbox, and other locations.

1. On a Mac, select one or more items, and then click the checkbox.

The "Quick View" window will open. If multiple items are selected, the first one is displayed.

2. In a quick window, do any of the following:
   - Add more glass windows: drag the corner of the glass window. Or click the "Full" button in the left corner of the "Quick Search" window. To leave the full screen, move the pointer under the window and press the full-screen button to exit.
   - Increase and decrease objects: Press Press-Plus (+) to enlarge the image, or Command-Minus (-) to decrease the image.
   - Turn items: press the left button and hold the Option key, then click the search page button. Keep clicking to continue editing items.
   - Mark the objects: click the mark button. View the markup file.
   - Cut audio or video: Click the "cut" button, then drag the yellow hand to the cut. To test your changes, click "Play". To restart, click resume. When you are ready to save your changes, click Finish and choose to edit the original file and create a new file.
   - View items (if you have selected several items): Click the flower near the left-hand side of the window, or click the left flower or keystroke. In full-screen mode, click the "Play" button to view

the project as a screenshot.
- Return items to the system (if you have selected multiple items): click the number table button and click Command-Return.
- Open the app: Click open with [App].
- Share the project: Click the share button, and then choose how to share the project.

3. When you're done, click the open bar or click the "Close" button to close the "Quick View" window.

When you open a live image in the "Quick View" window, the video clip of the image will automatically play. To find out more, click on the live image on the left-hand side of the image.

Keep your Mac up to date

Apple frequently releases macOS software updates (which add updates to apps that come with the Mac and key security legends).

If you receive a notification that a software update is available, you can choose when to install the update or choose to remind yourself the next day. You can manually check for macOS updates to the system requirements "Software Development".

Tip: To view the latest features of the app downloaded from the App Store, please open the App Store.

Checkmark for Mac update

To manually configure the update on your Mac, do any of the following:

- To download macOS software updates, select the Apple menu> "System Prefers" and click "Software Installation".

Tip: You can click on the Apple menu — the number of available updates (if available) will be displayed on the next page of "System Prefers". Select Web Preferences to continue.

- To update apps downloaded from the App Store, click on the Apple menu — the number of available updates (if available) will be displayed on the App Store page. Select "App Store" to continue the "App Store" app.

Set up your Mac to check for and check for software updates

1. On a Mac, select the Apple menu> "System Prefers" and then click "Change Software".
2. To install macOS updates, select "Automatically save on my Mac".
3. Set advanced configuration options, click Advanced, and then do one of the following:
   - To allow your Mac to check for updates, select "Check for Updates."
   - To not require you to download updates to your Mac, select "Download updates when available."
   - To properly configure your Mac to update macOS, select "Install macOS software."
   - To enable your Mac to install new apps from the App Store, select "Download applications from the App Store".
   - Simply download your Mac system files and security updates, select "Upload system data files and security updates."
4. Click OK.

To get the most up-to-date updates, you need to select "Check for updates", "Check for updates when available" and "Upload system database and security updates".

Note: MacBook, MacBook Pro must be installed and a MacBook Air with a power connector that automatically downloads updates.

Use touch ID on Mac

If the Mac has a Touch ID, you can use it to unlock the Mac, accept purchases from the iTunes Store, App Store, and Apple Books, and use Apple Pay to make purchases online. You can use Touch ID to access any of the three-page applications.

Set the touch ID

1. On a Mac, select the Apple menu> "System Prefers" and click "Touch ID".
2. Click "Add Fingerprint", enter the password, and follow the instructions on the screen.

You can add up to three fingers to your user account (your Mac can hold up to five fingers).

3. Click the checkbox to select how you want to use Touch ID:
   - Unlock Mac: wake up from sleep, use Touch ID to unlock this Mac.
   - Apple Pay: Use Touch ID to complete purchases made on this Mac using Apple Pay.
   - iTunes Store, App Store, and Apple Books: Use Touch ID to complete purchases from Apple's on-line store on Mac.
   - Keyword AutoFill: Use Touch ID to mechanically fill in user names and secret words and to automat-ically fill in credit card data when requested while using Safari and other apps.

Rename or delete the finger

1. On a Mac, select the Apple menu> "System Prefers" and click "Touch ID".
2. Do any of the following:
   - Rename a finger: Click the word under the finger,

    then enter a name.

- Wipe the finger: click the finger, enter the password, click OK, and then click Delete.

Use Touch ID to unlock Mac, log in or switch users

To use Touch ID for these functions, you must log in to your Mac by entering a password.

- Unlock your Mac and any password-protected devices: When you wake your Mac from sleep or unlock a password-protected device, simply stick your finger on the Touch ID when prompted.
- Log in from the login screen: press your name in the login screen, then place your finger on Touch ID.

The only user accounts with a password can be unlocked with Touch ID. Both users and users will not be able to use Touch ID.

- Switch users: click the quick switch user menu on the menu bar, select other users, and then place your finger on the Box ID.

To switch to another user using Touch ID, you must set the user switch speed, and the user to switch must be logged in to the Mac by logging in. a password.

Use Touch ID to purchase items

1. Log in to the Mac by entering the password.
2. Use Apple Pay or purchase goods from one of Apple's online stores.
3. When asked, put your finger on the ID Box.

See Using e-aa and Apple Pay on a Mac.

If you have trouble using Touch ID

- If Touch ID can't recognize your finger: clean and dry your finger, and try again. The fingertips can be wet, cut, cut, or peeled.

- If you need to enter a password: For security reasons, you need to enter a password when you start the Mac. Sometimes you need to enter a password to continue using Touch ID. For example, the user must re-enter the password after attempting five wrong fingers every 48 hours.

Note: to improve security, logged-in users can only access their Touch ID information. The administrator cannot change the preferences of Touch ID or the fingerprints of other users.

Use the touchpad on a Mac

If your Mac has a touch screen, you can use common features (such as tap, swipe, and swipe) directly on the touch screen to adjust settings, use Siri, enter task keys, and perform actions on other requests.

Control range

The push-button on the right side of the touch panel allows you to request Siri or easily customize the standard settings — just click a button, or for settings such as flash and voice, swipe quickly left and right. You can expand the navigation bar to get more buttons.

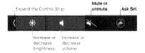

- Expand the navigation bar: Click the "Expand" button.

Depending on your Mac look and how you customize the touchpad, you can press and hold the Fn key or Globe key on the keyboard to expand the navigation bar.
- Use push buttons: press buttons to adjust settings or restrict video and playback. For some settings (such as the display flash), you can touch and hold the button

to change your setting.

- To collapse the chart: click the "Close" button.

Button request

The other buttons on the touch bar will change depending on the application you are using and the activity you are performing. Each application is different - try the "wall" to see what you can do.

For example, when you select a file in the Finder, there are buttons that you can click on.

Viewing photos in the "Photos" program, here are the buttons:

You can use the touch key to quickly add the emoji to the language in some programs. Just click the "Emoji" button, swipe to go through emojis (organized by category, such as "Frequently used" or "Emoji and People"), then click the emoji you want to use.

Tip: In some programs, you can customize the panel to add buttons for tasks you perform frequently.

Typing Suggestions

When typing a word on your Mac, the touch screen can display the words or phrases you want to use (called text suggestions) to help you save time.

- Display suggestions: click the "type in suggestions" button.

- Use input ideas: click on words, phrases, or emojis. Corrections are shown in blue.

- Hide entries: click the button next to the screen.

If you don't see the "Suggestions" button on the menu, choose View> Customize the actual panel, and then select "Show text comments." Or select the Apple menu> "System Prefers", click "Keyboard", "Text", and then select "Touch Bar Typing Preferences".

As you type, you can press F5 to display a list of expected words on the chart (you may need to press the Fn key, based on your mac configuration).

Colors

In applications where you can change the color of words or objects, you can use the touch bar to select the color, shade, and texture (e.g. with RGB or HSB).

- Select a color: Touch and hold the "Save" button, then slide your finger to a color.

- Select a shadow: click the "Save" button, touch and hold color, then slide your finger over the shadow.
- Select a color or color: click the color button, click the color list on the left, and then click a color type, such as RGB. To use a saved custom color, click "Swatches".

Use the slider to change the mode, such as hue or saturation. To keep track of changes to swatch, click the color (detected +), then click again (a checkmark appears).

- Hide color or color: click the "Close" button on the bar.

Action keys

Many macOS keyboard shortcuts use action keys (F1 to F12), such as F11 to indicate the keyboard. On a Mac with a touch key, the action keys are displayed on the touch screen.

1. To display the action keys on the touch panel, press and hold the Fn key or Globe key on the keyboard (applicable to the Mac model)\

Make sure to customize the keyboard to the liking of "Keyboard" which displays the action keys when the key is held down.

2. Click the action key.

If the keyboard shortcut contains switch keys (such as Option or Command), press the Fn and Globe keys and the switch keys. For example, use Control-F3 to move the Dock, press the Fn and Globe keys and the Control key at the same time, and then press F3 on the Dock.

Organize files in archives on Mac

You can use clusters on the desktop to organize files into groups. When you store a file on the desktop, the file is added to the appropriate stack to help keep the desktop clean. The Dock has a "download" section that lists the files you download from the Web.

Use the stack on the desk

You can group groups by category (such as image or PDF), date (such as business date or last opened date), or Finder searches. For example, all the documents on the table can be arranged in one batch, and screenshots can be combined into another batch.

On a Mac, you can do any of the following:

- Open the stack: Click on the desktop, then select Information> Use Stack or click Command-Command-0. You can hold down the Control key and click on the desktop, then select "Use Stack".
- Browse files in the stack: use two fingers on the trackpad to slide left or right on the stack; use one finger on the magic mouse. You can open the file above the archive by double-clicking it.
- To turn the stack on or off: Press the stack. You can double-tap a file to not built up it.
- Change how groups are grouped: Click on the desktop, select "View"> "Group By", and then select an option, such as "Add Date". Or press the Control key and click on the desktop, select "Group by", then select an option.
- Change the appearance of the stack: Click on the screen, select Information> Show options, and then change the options. Or press the Control key and click on the desktop, then select "Show Show options". You can make icons larger, change the spacing between icons, move icon labels to the page and display more information (for example, how many files are on the stack).

Use the stack on the Dock

The Dock comes with a "download" stack, which allows you to easily retrieve information downloaded from the Web, information received as an attachment and authorized using Air-Drop.

You can add files and folders to the Dock for quick access, and you can display them as a stack. The Mac will create an alias for the file or archive.

On a Mac, you can do any of the following:

- Combining files and folders: Drag and drop the file or archive to the right of the separator (after the previous application, if specified).

- Open or close a file or folder: click on it. After opening a file, double-click anything to open it. To view the file in Finder, click Open in Finder.
- Change the appearance of a folder: Hold down the Control key and click the folder, then choose how to separate the items, whether to display it in the Dock as a folder or a stack and how to know what they know (like a policeman or a wanderer).

Apple ID and iCloud

Create an Apple ID on a Mac

Apple ID lets you to right of entry the iTunes Store, App Store, Apple Books, iCloud, FaceTime, and other Apple services. He has an email address (e.g. michael_cavanna@icloud.com) and a password. Apple encourages you to use the same Apple ID for Apple services. To learn more about Apple ID, please visit the Apple ID support site.

You can create an Apple ID using your current email, or you can create an @icloud email for yourself.

You can create an Apple ID on a Mac, iOS, or iPadOS app, or on the Apple ID website. Please see the Apple support article to log in with your Apple ID.

Important: If you forgot or need to reset your Apple ID or password, please see the Apple support article If you forgot your Apple ID or forgot your Apple ID password.

Create an Apple ID using your current email address or an iCloud account created for you:

1. On a Mac, select the Apple menu> "System Prefers" and click "Login."
2. Click the Apple ID and follow the instructions on the screen.

> **Note:** in many countries and territories, you can use a phone number instead of an email address such as your Apple ID
> To learn how to set Apple ID preferences on a Mac, see Set Apple ID preferences on a Mac.

To ensure the security of your purchase and download of Apple services, please share your Apple ID and password with others. To share your purchases with your family, you can create a "family unit" of up to six family members. Find out What is family sharing?

For information about using Apple ID on iOS or iPadOS apps, see the "Manage Apple ID and iCloud Settings" in the iPhone, iPad, or iPod touch guide.

Use iCloud photographs to store pictures in iCloud

With iCloud photos, all photos and videos are stored in the photo archive on iCloud, so you can download them from Mac, PC, iPhone, iPad or Apple TV, and iCloud.com.

New photos and videos you add to "Photos" or taken from your iPhone or iPad will show up on all devices that search for "iCloud Photos". On each device, photos and albums are organized in the same way, and if you edit or delete items, you can see the changes across all devices.

Before setting up iCloud photos, please update to the latest version of macOS or the latest version of iOS or iPadOS on your device for info about using iCloud photos on a Windows PC, see the Apple support article on setting up and using iCloud photos on a Windows PC.

Open iCloud photos

If you are not logged in with your Apple ID, please select Apple menu> "System Prefers", click "Log in", and enter your Apple ID and password. Click iCloud on the Apple ID Preferences page, and then select images in the application list.

1. In the "Photos" app on your Mac, select "Photos"> "Preferences" and click "iCloud".
2. Check the "iCloud Photos" checkbox.

3. Choose one of the following options:
   - Download the source to this Mac: Store full images on Mac and iCloud.
   - Save the Mac archive: in the form of a storage limit, store small batches of images on the Mac, and store original images of many sources in iCloud. Select this option to save somewhere on your Mac. To restore the root to Mac, just select "Download root to this Mac".

When you open iCloud photos for the first time, it may take a while to upload the photos to iCloud. You can continue to use images while uploading them.

Tip: To take a break from uploading and downloading photos and videos uploaded using iCloud Photos, click on the library on the page, click a date on the task box, then click the pause button at the bottom of the information date. The upload is paused and downloaded for 24 hours, then resumed.

You can have many photo libraries, but iCloud Photos only stores photos and videos in the system's photo library today. Please browse the system art library and select the library as your photo library.

Prevent using iCloud Photos on Mac

You can transfer iCloud photos on your Mac without updating the photos between your Mac and other devices (for example, if you're selling or giving away your Mac).

Important Note: If you delete iCloud images, you will be prompted to select "Download source to this Mac" in the "iCloud" panel of the "Photos" preferences to only download all source images to your Mac. Before uploading iCloud photos, allow yourself time to download the original files. After uploading, your photos will be safely stored in "Photos", where you can use them, but they will never be uploaded to your other device.

1. In the "Photos" application on your Mac, select "Photos"> "Preferences" and click "iCloud".
2. Select the "iCloud Photos" checkbox.
3. Click Download to upload the photos to iCloud on your Mac, or click Download from Mac to delete any un downloaded photos and videos.

These will always be available to other apps that use iCloud.

After deleting iCloud photos, the edits you make to photos on your Mac will not be reflected on other devices. New images and videos will not be uploaded to Mac computers or devices on your Mac. Your photo archive is stored in iCloud and can be used by other users to access iCloud photos.

If you don't use iCloud Photos on your Mac, you can plug in your Mac and a connected iPhone or iPad to transfer photos. View synchronized images between Mac and iPhone or iPad.

Prevent the use of iCloud photos on all computers and devices

You can opt-out of using iCloud photos on Mac computers and devices, and not share the same pieces between them.

1. On a Mac, open Apple ID preferences in "System Prefers" and click iCloud on the landing page.
2. Click the Manage button, click the image, and then click "Close and Delete".

Tip: If you delete iCloud photos on all devices, your photos and videos will be deleted from iCloud within 30 days, unless you click "Undelete" before that time, it's not possible it is up to you to bring them back.

What is iCloud?

iCloud keeps track of your photos, videos, documents, music, applications, and more. and he always takes care of all the toys. With iCloud, you can share photos, calendars, places, and more with friends and family. If you lose your device, you can use iCloud to help you find it.

First, please sign in with your Apple ID to set up iCloud on Mac, iOS, and iPadOS apps, Apple Watch, Apple TV, and Windows computers.

To set up iCloud on an iOS or iPadOS app, Apple TV, or Windows computer, see how to set up iCloud on an iPhone, iPad, and iPod touch.

You can use iCloud in other ways.

iCloud features	Explain
store all your photos today on Mac, iOS TV and iCloud.com.	All photos and videos. Always available. iCloud Photos can securely and videos and store them apps, iPad OS apps, Apple

Edits you make to the
Photos app can be made

everywhere. Using shared
albums, you can

easily share photos and
videos with the people

you choose, and invite
them to add photos,

videos, and lyrics to the
album. shared. Learn

more about pictures.

• Download desktop and mobile apps for free

Use iCloud Drive to auto-
matically store your

desktop and document files
and folders in

iCloud so you can download
them on all devices

and iCloud.com. You can invite others to

work with you on the file.
You can use iCloud

sharing to share documents
with other iCloud

users who can handle files
and share changes

with you. Learn more

about iCloud Drive.

● Share songs, books, apps, subscriptions, and more with your family

The family allows you up to five family members to share purchases from the iTunes Store, App Store, and Apple Books, Apple Music family plan, iCloud storage plan, Apple News + and Apple Arcade subscription, etc.

Your family can share photos and family calendars, as well as help you find lost toys.

Learn more about family sharing.

Find out how to get rid of Mac

Use the "Find My" app to track down your Mac on the map, play a sound on it, lock its screen or

clear its data. Set up the
"Find My" app to find my

lost Mac.

With iCloud, your favorite apps are even better

Use the apps on Mac, iOS, and iPadOS
devices and

iCloud.com to keep your email, calendar, memos,

notifications, reminders, messages,
news, and files up

to date, and home kits help settings.
Learn more

about entry applications on the Mac.

ICloud browsers, bookmarks, and reading
lists in

Safari

View the web pages (your
iCloud accounts) you

open on your Mac, IOS, and iPadOS devices. Even

if you are not out, you can read
articles from the

reading list. Plus, it uses the same bookmarks on

Mac, iOS apps, iPadOS devices, and Openings

computers. Learn more about Safari.

ICloud keychain

Store passwords, credit card information, and

more, and automatically enter passwords on Mac,

iOS, and iPadOS devices. Learn more about iCloud

Keychain.

cloud storage

Each person has 5GB of free iCloud storage and

can be easily upgraded at any time. Your apps and

items purchased from the iTunes Store aren't

listed in your iCloud storage, so you'll need to use

them for things like photos, videos, files, etc., and

network supports. Learn more about iCloud

storage.

Note: iCloud requires a network connection; some iCloud features have low system costs. See the Apple support article for iCloud system requirements. iCloud may not be available in all countries: iCloud features may change from place to place.

Secure iCloud storage on Mac

Before you sign in with your Apple ID and built-up the iCloud selections, you automatically get 5 GB of free storage. Your iCloud storage is used for documents stored in iCloud folders, iCloud photos, iOS, and iPadOS network data, messages, and attachments in iCloud Mail (your @ iCloud email address). com), etc. If you don't have enough space, you can improve the deposit. You can delete saved items to provide more space

View and manage iCloud storage

1. On a Mac, select the "Apple"> "System Prefers" menu, click "Apple ID", and then select "iCloud" on the sidebar.
2. Click Manage, and then do one of the following:
   - Upgrade a space: click buy new space or change a storage plan, select where to save the space you want, and then follow the instructions.

   When you purchase an iCloud storage upgrade, it will be assigned a number on your Apple ID account. If you belong to a "Family Sharing" group and share a family purchase with the same Apple ID, the increase will be paid to the family organizer account.
   - Learn how to use an application or create a library: select the application or function on the left, then read the user information on the right.
   - Erase an iOS or iPadOS tablet: Click on the tablet

on the left, select the app that should not be supported on the right, and click Delete (below the tablet list). If you don't see "Desktop" on the left, that means your iOS or iPadOS app doesn't have an iCloud archive.

Warning: If you delete the iCloud database of the current iOS or iPadOS device, iCloud will stop supporting the device.
- Disable Siri and delete data about Siri: Select Siri on the left, then click "Disable and Delete".
3. Click Finish.

Delete items from the iCloud repository

You can completely delete all documents and information in the application, delete all documents, and restore files that have been deleted from iCloud Drive in the last 30 days. You can save a copy of the document and delete it from iCloud.

For information on adding Apple subscriptions, see the Apple support article "Get Apple One."

Set your preferences to Apple ID on Mac

Use your Apple ID to access your desired Apple ID. Your Apple ID gives you access to all Apple services, such as the iTunes Store, Book Store, App Store, iCloud, and other Apple services. After signing in, you can use Apple ID favorites to change your account name, picture, contact data, password and security settings, payment and carriage data, and more.

The Apple ID preferences page displays the different types of available account files, as well as the Overview preferences for existing files.

Use the subsequent pages to set up Apple ID favorites on your Mac:

- Overview: Use these options to review your

Apple ID and privacy policy and leave your Apple ID. Find out if you want an Apple ID.

- Name, phone number, email address: use these options to enter your name, phone number, email address, and other contact information related to your Apple ID. Get your Apple ID name, phone number, and email information.
- Password and security: Use these options to change the password and security settings associated with your Apple ID. Find out your password and Apple ID security information.
- Payment and Shipping: Use these options to set up payment and shipping information about your Apple ID.Set up your Apple ID payment method and shipment address.
- iCloud: Use these options to select the desired iCloud features and manage iCloud storage. See Configuring Apple ID iCloud settings.
- Media and purchases: use these options to exchange media and purchase settings related to Apple ID. See Set up your media Apple ID and purchase settings.
- Trusted devices: Use this list to view trusted devices that use the Apple ID, and to select and change options for trusted devices. View and manage your Apple ID credentials.

For information about changing Apple ID account information on the Apple ID website, please see the Apple ID account page.

To learn how to change Apple ID account settings using iOS or iPadOS apps, see "Manage Apple ID and iCloud Settings" on an iPhone, iPad, or iPod touch

Set up iCloud activity on Mac

After entering your Apple ID requirements, you can select

which iCloud activity you want to use each time.

ICloud options with all features selected.

Important: Set up Messages in iCloud to share instant messages between devices, open Messages on your Mac, select Messages> Your Preferences, click iMessage, and then select box Enable Messages in iCloud. See Using Messages in iCloud.

To set up iCloud features on an iOS or iPadOS app, Apple TV, or Windows computer, please see the Apple support article "Change iCloud feature settings".

Search or delete the iCloud function

1. On a Mac, select the "Apple"> "System Prefers" menu, click "Apple ID", and then select "iCloud" on the sidebar.
2. Select the application whose iCloud functionality you want to use. Select apps that do not have the iCloud features you want to use.

Some functions are available in other settings. You can change these settings by clicking on the option or the details next to the job name when the job opens.

If you select the "Contact" function when synchronizing the "Contact" program with Google Contacts, the Google Sync operation will be disabled. Using iCloud for connections, you need to stop.

Open iCloud photos

1. On a Mac, select the "Apple"> "System Prefers" menu, click "Apple ID", and then select "iCloud" on the sidebar.
2. select an image.

To learn more about setting up iCloud photos, see using iCloud photos.

Change iCloud keychain options

If your Apple ID is set to be used for two-factor authentication, after selecting the iCloud Keychain in the iCloud application list, the setup is complete. To set up iCloud on a new device, you will need to enter a password or password on the device that is set up with iCloud to allow the device to use iCloud data.

If an option button appears on the other side of the iCloud keychain option, follow the instructions below.

1. On a Mac, select the "Apple"> "System Prefers" menu, click "Apple ID", and then select "iCloud" on the sidebar.
2. Click the options button to connect to the keychain and select one of the following:
   - Maybe your iCloud keychain can be used to access the iCloud keychain on newer devices.
   - After using the iCloud security code, the iCloud security code and phone number are used to authenticate the information.
3. If "Waiting for Approval" appears under the key, click "Options" to enter your iCloud security code instead of approving this Mac from another device.

Change the search settings on my Mac

1. On a Mac, select the "Apple"> "System Prefers" menu, click "Apple ID", and then select "iCloud" on the sidebar.
2. If "Find location services" shows up under "Find my Mac," click "details" and follow the instructions on the screen to find the Mac.

To set up iCloud on an iOS or iPadOS app or a Windows computer, please see the Apple support article Setting up iCloud on an iPhone, iPad, or iPod touch.

Use iCloud file sharing to share files and official papers with other iCloud users

With iCloud sharing, you can share files and documents in iCloud Drive with other iCloud users. You and those you invite will be able to view and create your document. The person receiving the invitation can click the link to download the shared file or file from iCloud to one of their devices. Everyone sees the same things. If you allow other people to edit, they can edit the file, and the next time you open the file on your Mac, you'll see the update.

Note: To use iCloud Drive file sharing, your computer or device must have macOS 10.15.4 or higher, iOS version 13.4 or higher, or Windows version 11.1 or higher. iCloud.

To learn more about iCloud Drive and how to set it up on a Mac, see how to use iCloud Drive to store documents.

Archive or files

1. To share a file or document, do one of the following on your Mac:
   - In the Finder, select "iCloud Drive", select a file or document, click the "Share" button, and then select "Shared Folder" or "Shared File".

   Tip: If the item is on the desktop, right-click and click on it, then select "Share" from the shortcut menu, then select "Shared Folder" or "Shared File"
   - In an application that supports iCloud sharing, open a document, click the "Share" button, and select "Share File".
2. Select the application you want to use to send an invitation.

You can use "Mail", "Communication", "Copy Link" and "Airdrop" to send requests.

3. tap the "Who can access" pop-up list of options, and then do one of the following:

  - Select "Only invite people" to allow only invitees to access files or documents.

  - Select "Anything with a link" to allow those who have the link to download the archive or document. For instance, your invitees can share a link and give you the right to use it with others who are not in the original invitation.

4. Click the "Yes" pop-up menu and do one of the following:

  - The "Editable" option allows other people to edit items in the archive.

  - Select "View Only" to allow read-only images.

5. Click share and add the emails of the people you want to share with.

Once the host receives your invitation, they can download the shared archive or file from iCloud to one of their devices. If allowed, they can change the document, and you'll see the update the next time you open your file on your Mac.

If you only share a file with invited people, they will be able to access the files in the same file. To add more entries, you will need to change the settings of the section directory. You cannot change the settings of individual files in the archive.

Accept the invitation and change the document

When you download a file or document that you have been invited to share, you can see the shared file or file in other locations:

  - On iCloud Drive and Ma

  - "File" app on the device (iOS 11, iPadOS or higher) or iCloud Drive (iOS 10 or below)

  - With iCloud.co

  - On a PC with iCloud for Windows

If you are allowed to edit the document, you can remove it with any requests and then edit it.

1. In the invitation, click the link to the shared archive or document.

If necessary, please sign in with your Apple ID and password.

2. Open the document in a program on the Mac, edit it, and save it.

You can use any related application to open the document and make changes later. People who share a document will see the latest changes to the file the next time they open the file.

Change the analysis options of a file or document

You can change the delimitation settings of a delimited file or document at any time.

Note: You cannot change the sharing settings of a document in the same file. You need to change the file backgrounds.

1. On a Mac, select a file or document in the iCloud browser, or open it in an application that supports iCloud sharing.
2. Click the Share button, and then select Manage shared files or Manage shared folder.
3. Do any of the following:
   - Share the letter with more people: Click the "Add people" button, then add an email for each new invitee.
   - Copy the link to the provided file to send to others: ClickCopy link. Now you can paste the link into an email or another request.
   - Change who can download the file for download: From the "Who can access" pop-up menu, select "People you invite" to allow only invitees to access the document, file Who are the links to

download the document.

- Change if you can edit the shared document or just view the shared document: select "Can make changes" from the Pop-up permissions menu to allow users Others to edit the document, or select "View only".
- Change the sharing settings of a specific person: place the reference in the person's name, click it, and then select the desired setting.
- To stop sharing files with a specific person: enter the prompt in the person's name, click it, and then select Delete eAccess.

4. Click Finish.

Prevent sharing of files or documents

You can stop sharing files or files with people you invite.

1. On a Mac, select a file or document in the iCloud navigation, or open the document in an application that supports iCloud sharing.
2. Click the Share button, and then select Manage shared folder or Manage shared files.
3. Do any of the following:
   - Stop sharing with everyone else: Click Prevent sharing.
   - To stop sharing with a specific person: put the reference over the person's name, click it and select "Open photo."

You can move and delete files or documents from iCloud Drive to prevent others from retrieving them.

If you opt out or delete a shared archive, users will not be able to access files in that archive.

To delete files in an undivided file without changing copy settings, you can move files from the same repository.

Use iCloud Drive to store documents on Mac, iPhone, and iPad

With iCloud Drive, you can securely store various documents in iCloud and be able to download them from all computers as well as iOS and iPadOS apps. If you want, you can safely store all your files on the desktop as well as document files in iCloud Drive. This way, you can keep the files where they are always stored, and they are available on all computers as well as iOS and iPadOS apps.

You can use iCloud Drive on Mac laptops (OS X 10.10 or higher), iOS apps (iOS 8 or higher), iPadOS devices, and Windows laptops with iCloud for Windows (required) Windows 7 or higher). You must be logged in with the same Apple ID on all computers and devices.

You can use iCloud Drive on iCloud.com via the web browser on a Mac or Windows computer.

To use an iOS or iPadOS device, a Windows PC, or to set up an iCloud drive on iCloud.com, please see Apple's support article "Setting up an iCloud Drive".

Set up iCloud Drive

If you didn't set up iCloud Drive on this Mac, you can now set it up on the iCloud page of Apple ID preferences.

1. On a Mac, select the "Apple"> "System Prefers" menu, click "Apple ID", and then select "iCloud" on the sidebar.
2. Select "iCloud Drive".

The first time you choose the iCloud Drive feature on devices, you'll be asked to upgrade. Thankfully, documents and data will now be moved to iCloud in iCloud Drive. If you are not asked to approve, your account has been upgraded.

Important Note: After upgrading to iCloud Drive, only documents stored in iCloud Drive are available on computers that meet the minimum operating requirements and are converted to iCloud Drive, as well as iOS apps. and iPadOS. Your documents can be found in iCloud Drive at iCloud.com.

If you delete iCloud Drive apps, the documents and data on these devices will not be stored as well as the documents and information on the devices searched on iCloud Drive.

Store your Desktops and Documents in iCloud Drive

1. On a Mac, select the "Apple" menu> "Your Default Settings", click "Apple ID", select "iCloud" on the "iCloud Drive" page, and click "Options" on the "iCloud Drive" page.

If you don't see "options" for iCloud Drive, check to see if iCloud Drive is turned on.

2. Select desktop and document files.
3. Click Finish.

After selecting the "Desktop and Documents" folder, your "Desktop" and "Documents" will be moved to iCloud Drive. They can be found in the "iCloud Drive" section of the Finder page.

If you can't move and store documents in iCloud Drive

If you can't move and store documents in iCloud Drive, the iCloud space may be full. The document is stored on a Mac and uploaded to iCloud Drive when available.

iCloud Drive shares your iCloud storage with iCloud Photos, iOS and iPadOS dashboards, messages, and attachments in iCloud Mail (your email address at icloud.com).

Get more somewhere:

- Expand your library. View iCloud storage.
- Delete unnecessary items stored in iCloud Drive.

Mac hardware

Use the trackpads and gestures on the Mac

When you use an Apple trackpad or Magic Mouse on a Mac, you can use signs (such as click, tap, pinch, and slide) to zoom in on documents, browse music, or web pages, convert images, open the Warning Center, and more.

Touchpad functions

Use one or more fingers to press, tap, slide, slide, and so on. On the surface of the touchpad. For example, to move between the sheet of paper of a document, swipe left or right with two fingers.

- To see all the trackpad systems that can be used with your Mac, or to finish and adjust the movements, select Apple menu> "System Prefers" and click "Trackpad."

Mouse signal

Use one or more fingers to press, tap, slide, or slide the mouse. For example, to move between the sheet of paper of a document, swipe left or right with one finger.

- To see all mouse movements that can be used with a Mac, or to cancel or customize the movements, select the Apple menu> "System Prefers" and click "Mouse."

View battery usage history on a Mac laptop

View the user history to see the level of charts of your Mac notebook, how much power your Mac has consumed, and how long the screen has lasted. You can view the past 24 hours or the past 10 days.

1. Select the "Apple" menu> "System Prefers", click "Bat-

tery", and then click "Usage History".
2. Select the last 24 hours or the last 10 days to view the current usage history.
3. Check out some of these:
   - Level Interval: Displays the average level of interval every 15 minutes. The area covered shows when the computer is loading.
   - Energy Consumption: This shows how much energy your computer consumes daily.
   - Timing of use of the screen: Indicates how long the screen has been searched per hour or per day.

Fill in the blanks on Mac

macOS can release more space for Mac by verifying the Mac library. When space is needed, it stores files, photos and videos, Apple TV movies and TV shows, and email attachments to iCloud and delivers them on demand. The file doesn't take up space on a Mac, and you can download the original file if you need to. New files and ready-made controls of images on the Mac always.

1. Select the "Apple" menu> "About This Mac", click "Storage", and then click "Manage".

macOS calculates the amount of time used by different components.

Note: Please wait for the total area to be counted to make sure you know the correct size of the area. When each division is counted, the property is cleaned up.
2. Review the tips and decide how to add storage on your Mac

Store in iCloud

By storing only open files on your Mac when space is needed, it helps you store files and folders in the "Desktop" and "Documents" folders in iCloud Drive, and save photos and videos in iCloud Photo Library to store messages and attachments in iCloud

Use iCloud Drive to store official papers on Mac, iOS, and iPadOS apps", "Use iCloud pictures to store pictures in iCloud" and "Use Messages and iCloud ".

You can change these settings after iCloud preferences, "Photos" preferences, and "Messages" preferences.

Optimize system

Save space by deleting Apple TV movies and TV shows you've watched and keep only the most recent email attachments on this Mac where necessary.

Find out how to change the file preferences and message preferences in the TV program.

Just throw out the trash

Be sure to remove items in the trash for at least 30 days. You can change this setting in the Finder later. See Delete Files and Folders.

Reduce confusion

Quickly find files, applications, books, movies, and more, and clean up unwanted content. Search and delete files.

When space is needed on the Mac, macOS also clears caches and sections that can be safely erased, such as temporary archive files, terminated downloads, macOS timelines, and installations. updates of the application, as well as Safari web data.

Note: If the screen is detached, it should only attach to the screen that has the home directory.

To get an overview of the sites used and available, select "Apple"> "About This Mac" menu, then click click "Storage". Make sure you have a secure system.

Use Bluetooth software on Mac

Bluetooth lets you establish short wire connections (up to 30 feet) among your Mac and devices such as smartphones and peripherals.

Use the Bluetooth solution of Internet Preferences to connect to other Bluetooth applications. On a Mac, select the Apple menu> "System Prefers" and then click "Bluetooth."

Using Bluetooth, you can:

- Use a flashlight, mouse, or trackpad
- Use Bluetooth headsets on your computer
- Share files using Bluetooth
- Use a Bluetooth -enabled printer
- Use a mobile phone that can link to the Internet

Burn CD and DVD on Mac

If your Mac has a built-in visual drive, or an external DVD drive (such as an Apple USB SuperDrive) is uninvolved, you can burn files to CDs and DVDs to share the same files. files with friends, move files between laptops, or make backup files. The stars you burn on your Mac can be used on Windows and other types of computers.

1. Put ina blank CD into the CD drive.

If you see a dialog box, click on the pop-up menu and select "Open Finder". If you want to open the Receiver each time you insert a blank disk, select "Do this operation as default."

The CD is on your desktop.

2. Double-click the disk to open its window, and then drag the files and folders you want to open the window.

The alias of the file is in the CD window. The unique file will not be moved or erased.

Note: If you want to burn the same file to a disk multiple times, please use the burn file.

3. Organize and rename files.

Burning a disc, the objects on the disc have the same name and location as the window. After the disc has been burned, you will not be able to change anything.

4. choose"File"> "Burn [Disc]" and follow the directives.

The file specified by the offering will be burned to disk. In addition, if the file is attached to a disk with namespaces, the files pointed to by those names will be burned on the disk.

Note: If you eject the disc without rooting it, a backup will be created that contains the contents of the copy to the disc and placed on the desktop. To complete the burning process, click the burn icon on the archive page on the Finder page, or press the Power key while clicking on the tabs, and select Burn Disc from the menu bar.

Burn a disk image (.dmg file) to a disk, press the Power key and click the disc image file, then select "Burn image [disk name] to disk" from the short menu, then follow the directions.

Tip: To clear the contents of a rewritable disc, press the Control key on the Finder page and click on the CD or DVD player, then select "Erase Rewritable Disc" from the menu directory.

Use the camera built into your Mac

Many Mac laptops and monitors have built-in FaceTime or FaceTime HD cameras near the top of the display. Click the photo booth when you open an application (such as FaceTime, Messaging, or Photo Booth) or use functions that can be used by the camera (such as a marker or head pointer). allows you to decide which applications are allowed to use the camera on the Mac. See image compression in the clipboard.

- Turn on the camera: On a Mac, open an application or open an activity that can use the camera. The green light near the camera indicates that the camera is turning.
- Turn off the camera: On a Mac, turn off and exit all applications, or turn off all activities that can use the camera. The green light near the video camera turns off, indicating that the camera is off.

To study more about using the camera thru the above-mentioned requests, please refer to the "FaceTime User Guide", "Message User Guide" and "Photo Booth User Guide".

Connect Apple wireless devices to your Mac

To use Apple's tablet, mouse, or trackpad, you'll need to connect the device to your Mac to access Bluetooth.

Add Magic Control panel, Magic Mouse 2, and Magic Trackpad 2 to Mac

When you attach your keyboard, mouse, or trackpad to your Mac, it automatically links to your Mac via Bluetooth.

- Link one end of the USB cable to the Magic Control panel, Magic Mouse 2 or Magic Trackpad 2, and the other end to the USB port on your Mac. On your Mac, you may need an appendix, which can be downloaded from the Apple Store or at apple.com.

You can use Magic Keyboard or Magic Trackpad 2 when connected to a Mac. Once connected, you will not be able to use Mouse 2.

When you use Bluetooth to connect your keyboard, mouse, or trackpad to your Mac, you'll get a notification telling you that you can disconnect the cable and use the device without it.

Connect an Apple Keyboard, Magic Mouse, or Magic Trackpad to your Mac

To make sure the file has been downloaded, the keyboard, mouse, or trackpad is properly inserted, and the device is turned on and visible.

1. On a Mac, select the Apple menu> "System Prefers" and then click "Bluetooth."
2. Select the keyboard, mouse, or trackpad from the "Anything" list, then click "Connect".

If you want to replace the chart on the keyboard, mouse, or trackpad, press the mouse or trackpad or press the key on the keyboard to reconnect it to the Mac.

For more help with using Bluetooth, click the "Help" button in Bluetooth preferences.

Connect a monitor, TV, or projector to the Mac

You can use one or more of the other options to connect your Mac to a monitor, TV, or program.

- Connect the monitor to the USB-C port: Use a Thunderbolt 3 (USB-C) cable to connect the monitor to the USB-C port on the Mac. For older monitors, use a multiport USB-C digital AV adapter or a USB-C VGA multiport adapter to connect the monitor to the USB-C port on your Mac.
- Connect a monitor, TV, or programmer with an HDMI interface: connect the device's HDMI cable directly to the Mac's HDMI port. To learn more about how to install a TV, see how to use a TV as a monitor on a Mac.
- Connect a monitor or device to a VGA port: Use a Mini DisplayPort to VGA connector to connect the monitor

to the Thunderbolt port on a Mac.

- Connect the viewer to the Mini DisplayPort: Connect the cable directly to the Mini DisplayPort on the Mac.
- Connect Apple Pro Display XDR: Connect the monitor's Thunderbolt 3 Pro cable to the Thunderbolt 3 (USB-C) or Thunderbolt / USB-4 port on the Mac. See the Apple support article "Setting up and using Apple Pro Display XDR".
- Connect the Apple Thunderbolt display: Connect the display cable directly to the Thunderbolt port on the Mac. For newer Mac computers, use the Thunderbolt 3 (USB-C) to Thunderbolt 2 adapter to connect the monitor to the Mac.
- Connect Apple LED Cinema Display: Connect the display cable directly to the Mini DisplayPort or Thunderbolt 2 port on your Mac. Newer Mac computers do not support this feature.

If your viewer uses a video port that is not available on your Mac, you can use an adapter to connect to the monitor.

Family and friends on macOS

Compose and send email messages on Mac

Writing a message, you can attach the contents, the message, photos, and more before sending the message.

1. In the "Mail" program on your Mac, click the "New Mail" button on the "Mail" toolbar (or use the touch screen).

Ask Siri. Say something like: "Send Katie about the tour information." Learn how to ask Siri.

To add people or accessories, or to advance your message, double-click the Siri window to open it in Mail.

2. In your message, include the person you want to send it to.

Use other fields, such as "Bcc" or "Priority", click the "title" button and then click a field.

3. Enter the subject of the message, then add your own.

You can do any of the following:

- Click the Format button (or use the touchpad) to quickly change the font and style.
- Click the emoji button (or use the related bar) to easily combine emojis and symbols.
- Change the wording or use text ideas (if available).
- Click the attach button or the image view button to attach an image or document.
- Draw attachments - for example, write on attach-

ments, draw or cut attachments, and so on. Or hold down the Control key and click anywhere on the body of the letter, then select "Insert Drawing" to use the drawing tool to insert your drawings or drawings.
- Add your email address.
4. When you are ready to send the message, click the send button (or use the touch bar).

If you use the "switch", you can start the message in "Mail" on another device, and then end the message in "Mail" on your Mac. To continue composing a delivered message to the Mac, click the Handoff Mail icon that appears on the left side of the screen.

What is family sharing?

Family allows up to six members of your family to share items purchased from the iTunes Store, App Store, and Apple Books, family calendar, family memorial board, and family photos without sharing. archives. Your family can share subscriptions for Apple Music, Apple TV, Apple News +, etc.

The "Family Sharing" preferences page shows the different types of history options available, as well as the "family" families for existing files.

A parent (family organizer) sets up "Family Sharing", invites 5 people to join the "Family Sharing" group, and selects activities for your family to share. Family members can quickly download music, movies, TV shows, books, relevant apps, subscriptions to Apple TV and Apple News +, and more. In addition, family members can easily share photos of similar family albums, add events to the family calendar, share memories, share their location with other family members, as well as help you find other family members' toys. After the family reunites, "Family Sharing" will be set up on everyone's device.

Each member of the family needs an Apple ID and must access

their Apple ID preferences to access "Family Sharing" benefits. For very young children to create an Apple ID, the family organizer can provide parental consent and create an Apple ID in the child's name while adding the child to the family. Family separation is used for the same family (parents and children). You can become a member of the family analysis group at any time.

To set up a family sharing organization, you must first sign in to the Apple ID requirements with your Apple ID. Then the "Home Sharing" options will appear in "System Prefers." Click on family sharing, and then, as the family organizer, organize your family area. Learn how to set up home sharing on a Mac.

Home sharing is available on Mac computers (OS X 10.10 or higher), iOS apps (iOS 8 or higher), iPadOS apps, and Windows computers with iCloud for Windows (Windows 7 and higher required) thigh). For information about setting up Family Giving on iOS apps and iPadOS devices, see the Apple Support article "Setting up Family Giving.

Track down a friend in finding me on Mac

After you start subsequent your friends, you can view and mark their whereabouts, call them via email, FaceTime or email, and get directions to their location.

Ask Siri. Words like: "Where is John Bishop?" Or "Who's next?" Learn how to ask Siri.

1. In "See my apps" on your Mac, tap "People".
2. In the list of people, select a name.
   - If you can see your friends: They show on the map, so you can see their location.
   - If you can't find your friend: See "Places Not Found" under their name.
   - If you don't follow your friends: you'll see "You can see where you are" under their names. Ask to follow friends to check their location.

3. Click the "Info" button on the map, then do one of the following:
   - Add a label to a friend's place: Click "Edit place name" and select an option (such as "family" or "Gym"), or click "Add fun name", enter a name, and click enter.

The label will be displayed under your friend's name instead of the location information.

Ask Siri. Say something like: "Is John working?" Learn how to ask Siri.

   - Join with friends: Click Join, and then select an option.

Note: You can hold down the Control key and click the name in the "People" menu, then select "Show Contact Card".

   - Get directions to your friend's place: Click on the path.

Note: You can hold down the Control key and click the name in the "Person" menu, then select "Direction".

Open the "Maps" app and show a route from your place to your friend's. See directions on the map.

   - Set up notifications: Learn how to set up notifications for friends.

Set up home sharing on Mac

The family allows six members of your family to share purchases from the iTunes Store, App Store, and Apple Books, as well as iCloud storage plans -no sharing of archives. Your family can share Apple Music, Apple TV, Apple News +, and Apple Arcade subscriptions (not available nationally or locally). Your family can use the "Find My App" on Mac, iCloud.com, and iOS and iPadOS devices to help find each other's apps.

The "Family Sharing" preferences page shows the different types of history options available, as well as the "family" families for existing files.

A parent (family organizer) organizes "Family Sharing" and invites five people to join the "Family Sharing" group. To learn more about family sharing, find out what family sharing is all about.

To set up home sharing with an iOS or iPadOS device, see the Apple support article "Set up home sharing."

1. On a Mac, select the Apple menu> "System Prefers" and do one of the following:
   - If you already have your Apple ID: Tap to share with family.
   - If you are not logged in and do not have an Apple ID: click Login, and follow the instructions on the screen (enter your Apple ID and click Create Apple ID if you do not have one). After signing up, click "System Preferences" at the top of the Settings window, and then click "Family Sharing" next to "Apple ID Prefers." "
2. Click to start, then invite others to join the "Family Sharing" group.
   - Invite family members: Click on the person who invited and follow the prompts on the screen

If the person you want to invite is nearby, you can select "Call person" and ask them to enter their Apple ID and password on the Mac. If not, you can use email, mail, or AirDrop to send the invitation.

If the person you are inviting does not have an Apple ID, they will need to create an Apple ID before they can accept your invitation.

   - Create an Apple ID for younger children: Click Create a child account and follow the instructions on the screen. Please see the Apple support article about sharing your child's family and Apple ID.

3. To add more family members to the "Share family" group, click the "Add" button and follow the instructions on the screen.

4. Do any of the following:

- Set up location-allocation: select "Share Location" on the page, then click "Learn More" to learn how to set location-allocation on all devices. You can set up sharing so family members can find their location in "Find My App" and "Messages." You can use the "Find Me" app on Mac, iCloud.com, iOS, and iPadOS apps.

- Set up sales sharing: select "Sales" on the sidebar. If you have already set up a payment method, click "Set up purchase sharing". If not, click "Add a paid action" and follow the instructions on the chart. Your family can share purchases from the iTunes Store, App Store, and Apple Books so everyone can access them. All purchases are made through the same payment process that you set up. You can change the library used to make the purchase or refuse to share your purchase with your family.

- Share or upgrade iCloud storage: select "iCloud Storage" on the page, then share your 200 GB or 2 TB iCloud storage or add a shared storage with your family. Family members can share the plan with you or manage their care program.

- Set "Want to Buy": Tap "Want to Buy" on the landing page, then Tap "Open to Buy". This setting requires children in your family group to have your permission to download or purchase items from the App Store, iTunes Store, or Apple Books.

- Set the timeout: select "Timeout" on the sidebar, click "Set Timeout Time", and then select the desired option.

- Find the subscription service you want to share: select "Apple Subscription" on the landing page and click "Learn More" for the service you want to purchase.

Before family members can purchase, everyone must register the Apple piece purchased from the iTunes Store, App Store, and Apple Books. Find out how to share your purchases with others in the "Family Sharing" section.

For information on adding Apple subscriptions, see the Apple support article "Get Apple One."

Create your Memoji with memos on Mac

With macOS Big Sur, create a personal Memoji to match your style. Then, send Memoji stickers to show your style in the email.

1. In the "Messages" program on your Mac, select Conversations.
2. On the left side of the field at the bottom of the window, click the "Apps" button and then select the "Memoji Stickers" button.
3. Click the "Add" button, then follow the instructions on the screen to customize Memoji, starting from the skin to the headgear.
4. Click Finish.

Send messages on Mac

You can send a message to one person or a group of people (meet these requirements). Messages can include words, pictures, videos, voice memos, endpoints, Memoji stickers, etc. If you are using macOS 10.15 or later, iOS 13 or later, or iPadOS 13 or later, you can send messages to businesses.

Note: Before sending messages, you need to set up your Mac to send messages.

Ask Siri. Say this:

- "Tell mom I'm late"
- "The answer is good news"

Learn how to ask Siri.

Send a note to one or more people

1. In the "Messages" program on your Mac, click the "Compose" button to start a new message (or use the touch screen).
2. Type a name, email address, or phone number for each person you want to send a message to in the "To" field. As you type in your information, "message" indicates that it matches the address in the "Contact" program or the address of the person you previously sent the message to.

You can click the "Add" button on the right side of the "To" field. Click a link in the list, then an email or phone number.

If you can only send and accept messages with certain individuals, an hourglass icon will appear about who you can't send messages to.

3. Insert your message in the field at the bottom of the window. You can consist of any of the subsequent:
    - Text: Enter the word in the message field. You can use text comments (if any).

Tip: Click the Option-Return key to insert a line break in the message.

- Record Audio: click the "Record Audio" button to send an email.
- Emoji: Click the "Emoji Selector" button (or use the touch bar) to add the emoji to your message. If you add three or fewer emojis, they will be displayed as a large emoji.
- Photos: tap the "Apps" button, then choose the "Photos" button. See how to send pictures from the museum.
- Memoji Stickers: Click the Apply button, then select the Memoji Stickers button. Learn how to use Memoji and #images stickers.
- #images: Click on the "Applications" button, then select the #images button. Learn how to use Memoji and #images stickers.

Note: Images and GIFs will not be sent to any country or region.

- End of the message: click the "Request" button, then select the "End Control" button. See Using Message Ends.
- File or Weblink: Drag and copy and paste the file or Web link.

4. Press the return key on the keyboard and press the "Send" button to send the message.

You can create a reminder when you receive a message asking to do an action at a specific time or asking you to provide an answer. For example, if someone sends this message:

- "Call me at 6:00 PM": Hold down the Power key and click the checked text, then select "Create reminder."
- "Can you drink some milk tomorrow? Once replying "Yes" (or alike), memory will be displayed that is normal below Siri's mind. in the "Reminder" program.

Learn to add, change or delete memories.

Use words in conversations

With macOS Big Sur, you can tell other people in the conversation to draw their attention to specific messages. According to their arrangement, he would let them know if they were being rude.

The language can be used when using iMessage.

1. In the "Messages" program on your Mac, select a conversation.

To search for contacts and information in conversation, click on the "Search" field on the left-hand side and enter what you're looking for. Alternatively, choose from suggested links, images, and more.

If you can just send and receive messages with some, an hourglass icon will appear about who you can't send messages to.

2. Start by typing the name of the contact in the message field at the bottom of the window.

After entering the person's name, the name will be spelled over him or her, then select the name of the conversation as it appears.

You can also say @ in the message, then enter @, then enter the name of the attachment.

To change your advertising preferences when you are prompted for "Messages", go to "Messages"> "Preferences", click "General", and select (or select) "Notify me when my name is spoken. " "Look at how to save messages from emails.

Reply to a specific message in a conversation

With macOS Big Sur, you can reply to specific messages in online conversations to improve clarity and help keep the conversation going.

Using iMessage, you can use customized replies.

1. In the "Messages" program on your Mac, select a conversation.

To search for contacts and information in conversation, click on the "Search" field on the left-hand side and enter what you're looking for. Alternatively, choose from suggested links, images, and more.

If you can only send and accept messages with certain persons, an hourglass icon will appear about who you can't send messages to.

2. Right-click the message or attachment, then select "Reply" or press Command-R (or use the related bar).
3. Enter your message in the field at the bottom of the window and click Return on the keyboard and click the Send button.

Move the message or attachment

You can send messages (or attachments, such as pictures or videos) during the chat.

1. In the "Messages" program on your Mac, select a conversation.

To search for contacts and information in conversation, click on the "Search" field on the left-hand side and enter what you're looking for. Alternatively, choose from suggested links, images, and more.

If you can only send and receive emails with certain persons, an hourglass icon will appear about who you can't send messages to.

2. Hold down the Control key and click the message or attachment, then select "Forward".
3. Add the contents and click Enter.

The message or attachment has been sent.

You cannot send messages to people who are restricted by conversation restrictions in "Timeout".

Send a message to the business

If you are using macOS 10.15 or later, iOS 13 or later, or iPadOS 13 or later, you can send messages to certain services. A business consultant can help you get answers to questions, solve problems, get advice, buy Apple Pay to make purchases, etc.

1. On your Mac, use Google Maps to find the business you want to talk to or remove an email from that business.

See a location on the map.

2. To start the conversation, click on "Messages" in the "Geographic Information" tab, or click on the link in the email.

If this is the first time you have sent a message to this service, a new conversation will be created. If not, you can continue the conversation.

You cannot send messages to activities that are prohibited by conversation restrictions during "Time".

3. Enter your message in the field at the bottom of the window and press Enter. You can enter some of the same information when sending messages to other people.

Note: Business emails that you send are shown in gray to separate them from iMessage (blue) and emails or SMS or MMS (green).

Setting SMS forward, Mac can receive and send SMS and MMS messages via iPhone. For example, if a friend sends you an email from a phone other than the iPhone, the message will be displayed in the "messages" of the Mac and iPhone.

Note: To obtain and send SMS and MMS messages on Mac, your iPhone requires iOS 8.1 or later, and your iPhone and Mac must use the same Apple ID to access iMessage. In addition, you need to configure your iPhone.

Set safe time for kids on Mac

The easiest and easiest way to set up and maintain time management for children is to use "Family Sharing". When using Family Sharing, you can navigate and monitor how each child uses his or her personal use on Mac, iPhone, or iPad. However, if you don't use family sharing, you can set up time control for your child by logging into your child's Mac account.

The response of time control and time control options is the same. Select system data and use the "Password Timeout" option.

1. On a Mac, do any of the subsequent:
   - If you use Family Sharing: Log in to your Mac user account, then make sure you log in with your Apple ID.
   - If you don't use family sharing: Log in to your child's Mac user account.
2. Choose Apple menu> Your Site Settings, and click Timeout.
3. If you are using Family Sharing, click the pop-up menu on the right side of the page and select a child.
4. Click on the option on the left side of the page.
5. Click Search in the upper right corner.
6. Choose one of the following options:
   - Add website data: Select this option if you want the time report to include detailed information about visited websites. If this option is not selected, the site will only be displayed as a Safari

user.

- Use time password: Select this option to prevent the time setting from being changed and require the password to reset the time when the restriction expires.

7. If you wish, do one of the following:

- Click "Downtime" on the sidebar, and then set the downtime schedule.
- Click "Application Limits" on the page, and then set the time limit for the application and the system.
- Click on the conversation on the page, and then set the conversation limit.
- Click "Permissions" on the page, and then select a program that you can use at any time.
- Click Information and Privacy on the page, and then set settings and privacy.

Make FaceTime calls on Mac

You can make FaceTime calls to one or more users who have Mac, iOS, or iPadOS devices that meet these requirements. Face-Time calls use Wi-Fi or network data.

Ask Siri. Languages like this:

- "Mommy mommy"
- "FaceTime Voice [Phone Number]"

Learn how to ask Siri.

You can use the Internet connection near your iPhone to make calls to anyone directly from your Mac. See Make and receive calls on FaceTime.

Call FaceTime

1. In the FaceTime app on the Mac, log in and verify that FaceTime is detected.
2. In the pitch at the top of the FaceTime window, enter the email address or phone number of the person you want to call. You need to click back.

If you have the person's business card in the "Contacts" program, you can enter the person's name. To learn more about joining a group, see Create a relationship with Face-Time.

Note: If you are limited to only making calls to certain people, the hourglass icon will appear next to the people you can't call.

3. To initiate a FaceTime call, press the "Video" button or the "Audio" button (or use the touch panel).

If you press the "Audio" button and set it to make calls on your Mac, you can choose whether to make FaceTime voice calls or make calls. When you make a call or make a call, the camera will not turn off.

4. When making a call, you can change the call perception, pause it, mute it or change the volume of the call, or connect more people to the FaceTime phone.

If you made a rejected or unanswered video call, you can click the "Message" button to send someone to iMessage (you need to log in to iMessage).

Call a FaceTime group

In a FaceTime group call, you can call up to 32 people at the same time. (See FaceTime group requirements.)

1. In the FaceTime app on the Mac, log in and verify that

FaceTime is detected.

2. In the field at the top of the FaceTime window, enter the email address or phone number of the person you want to call. You need to click back.

If you have the person's business card in the "Contacts" program, you can enter the person's name. For information about merging companies, learn how to use FaceTime to create relationships.

Note: If you are limited to only making calls to certain people, the hourglass icon will appear next to the people you can't call.

3. Repeat step 2 until all participants are listed.
4. To initiate a FaceTime call, press the "Video" button or the "Audio" button (or use the touch panel).

If you press the "Audio" button and set it to make calls on your Mac, you can choose whether to make FaceTime voice calls or make calls. Whether you are making a Face-Time voice call or a mobile phone, the camera will immediately turn off.

Each entry represents a block on the chart. When a member says or you click on a tile, the tile will move forward and become popular. The unmatched tiles on the chart are displayed in a row at the bottom of the screen. To find items you don't see, scroll down the row.

Tip: If you don't like people who talk a lot, you can uncheck the FaceTime preferences. Select "FaceTime"> "Your News Settings", click "Options", and then select chat under the upper level.

To send notifications to callers who have not entered a call, click the "Sidebar" button, and then click "Ring."

During a call, you can change the feel of the call, pause, mute, or change the volume of the call.

Add more people to FaceTime calls

When you make a FaceTime call, you can connect more people (up to 32 people) to the phone even if you have not initiated the call. (See FaceTime group requirements.)

1. In the FaceTime app on the Mac, make and enter a FaceTime call or FaceTime call.
2. Click the sidebar button.
3. Click the "Add Person" button and enter the email or phone number of the person you want to call. If you have the person's business card in the "Contacts" program, you can enter the person's name.

Note: If you are limited to only making calls to certain people, the hourglass icon will appear next to the people you can't call.

4. Click Add.

Each entry represents a block on the chart. When a member says or you click on a tile, the tile will move forward and become popular. The unsuitable tiles on the screen display a line at the bottom of the screen. To find items you don't see, scroll down the row.

Tip: If you don't like people who talk a lot, you can uncheck the FaceTime preferences. Select "FaceTime"> "Your News Settings", click "Options", and then select chat under the upper level.

To send notifications to callers who have not entered a call, click the "Sidebar" button, and then click "Ring."

During a call, you can change the feel of the call, pause, mute, or change the volume of the call.

End the call

In the FaceTime app on your Mac, do any of the following to end the call:

- End voice mail: Click the Enable Notification button.
- End a video call: Move the prompt in the window and press the "End Call" button (or use the touch bar).

After finishing the FaceTime group call, it will continue to work and the caller will leave the phone. To join again, click the video join button.

Share procurements with others in the "Family Shares" group

As a family member, you can quickly access purchases that are shared with other family members. You can download purchased goods on your computer, iOS, and iPadOS devices at any time. You can allow other family members to make your purchases in the same way. You can hide personal purchases if you don't want other family members to share them.

Before setting up a family sale, you need to join the "Family Sharing" group and set up a "Sharing Sign".

For information on changing home-sharing settings using an iOS or iPadOS app, see the Apple support article "Shared App Store, iTunes Store, and Apple Books Purchased" through Family Sharing. "

To learn how to change the "Family sharing" settings in the "Music" application, see "Using family sharing to share iTunes purchases of songs.". "

View and copy purchases made by other family associates

1. Go to the "Sold" section in "Music", "App Store" or "Apple Books".
   - In the music: select Account> Purchased. If you do not see the command prompt, please select "Account"> "Login".
   - In the App Store: select "Store"> "View my account. If you do not see the command line, please select" Store ">" Login ".

- In "Books": Select "Buy"> "Bookstore", and click "Buy" under "Quick Links" on the right.
2. Click on your name or select a family member to see their purchase.
3. Download the required items.

When a family member starts a sale, he or she is donated directly to the family planning fund. After purchase, the product will be added to the starting family member's account and shared with other families. If the family planner stands for family sharing, then everyone will take care of what they choose to buy, even if the family planner pays for it. For information about purchasing iCloud enhancements, see Managing iCloud Storage.

Hide purchases from other family members

You can hide your purchased music, App Store, and Apple Books so those other family members cannot use them.

1. Go to the "Sold" section of "Apple", "App Store" or "Apple Books".
    - In the music: select Account> Purchased. If you do not see the command prompt, please select "Account"> "Login".
    - In the App Store: select "Store"> "View my account.
    - In "Books": Select "Buy"> "Bookstore", and click "Buy" under "Quick Links" on the right.
2. Do any of the following:
    - In "Music": select the type of information you want to hide, place the pointer on what you want to hide, click the "Clear" button, then click "Hide".
    - In the App Store: place the cursor on what you want to hide, click the "show more" button, select "hide sales", and then click "hide sales".
    - In "Books": Place the instruction on the product to hide, click the "Delete" button, then click

"Hide".

Prevent secret sales

You can reveal your hidden items purchased from each Music, App Store, and Apple Books for other family members to use.

1. Navigate to the "Information" tab in "Music", "App Store" or "Apple Books".
   - In the menu: select Account> View My Account. If you do not see the command prompt, please select "Account"> "Login".\
   - In the App Store: select "Store"> "View my account. If you do not see the command line, please select" Store ">" Login ".
   - In "Books": select "Store"> "See my Apple ID". If you do not see the command line, please select "Store"> "Login".
2. Do any of the following:
   - In "Music": Tap "Hidden Purchases", click "Manage", then click "Unhide".
   - In the App Store: Click for info. In the hidden areas, click Manage, and then click Unhide.
   - In "Books": Tap "Hidden Purchases", click "Manage", and then click "Unhide" for the product.

Stop sharing your purchase

When you stop sharing purchases, your family will not be able to download shared iTunes Stores, Apple Books, and App Store purchases, and will not be able to do so. similar new sales.

1. On a Mac, select the Apple menu> "System Prefers", click "Family Sharing", and then select "Family Sharing" on the sidebar.
2. Under your account information, deselect Share my purchases.

For information on adding Apple subscriptions, see the Apple support article "Get Apple One."

Note: To share purchases, family members must be on the iTunes Store or locally. a. If a family member changes their iTunes Store location or section, that person will not be able to access other family members' purchases, and requests submitted with other family members will be processed. Please see the Apple Support article to change your Apple ID country or region.

Apps

Open programs and documents on Mac

There are many and many wrong ways to open applications and documents.

Open the program

On a Mac, do any of the following:

- Use Siri: Siri will open the application for you. Say something like "open."
- Use the Dock: Click the application icon on the screen.
- To use the launch pad: Click the launchpad icon in the Dock (or use the navigation bar), then click the application icon.
- Use the Flashlight: Open a flashlight, enter the name of the request in the search field, and click Return.
- To use the finder: tap the Finder icon in the Dock, click "Applications" on the Finder page, and then double-tap the Application icon
- Use the "New Users" menu: select the "Apple" menu> "New Users", then select the application.

Open a document

On a Mac, do any of the following:

- Use Siri: Siri will open the document. Words like "Open My File Kitchen Remodel".
- In an application: For some applications, when you open the application, an "Open" dialog box will appear. If you do not see the Open dialog box, select File> Open. View the document (you may need to refer to the page to see other files), select it, and click "Open".

In some applications, you can open the most recent document by selecting "File"> "Open this document" and then

selecting the document.
- On the desktop: If there is a document icon on the desktop, double-click the document icon.
- Use Spotlight: Open a spotlight, enter the name of the document in the search field, and then double-click the document.
- To use the finder: click the Finder icon on the screen. On the Finder sidebar, click "Latest Records", "iCloud Drive", "Documents" or the archive instead of the document, and then double-click the icon or document name.

Note: To open a document in iCloud Drive, you need to turn on the iCloud Drive function. See Use iCloud Drive to Store Documents.
- Use the "Updates" menu: select the "Apple"> "Updates" menu, then select the document.

Download products purchased from the App Store on Mac

There are many, many ways to install and reinstall apps purchased with Apple ID.

Note: In the App Store, all your purchases are tied to your Apple ID and cannot be transferred to another Apple ID. If you shop on an iPhone, iPad, or other Mac, always sign in with the same Apple ID so you can see in-store purchases on this Mac and download updates to in stock.

Download the software you have purchased on other devices

You can upload any purchased application with Apple ID on another device.

1. In the App Store on your Mac, click your name on the left-hand side, or if you're logged in, click "login".
2. Find the purchased application you want to download and click the "Download" button.

Automatically download apps you have purchased on other

devices

1. In the App Store on your Mac, click your name on the left-hand side, or if you're logged in, click "log in".
2. Select "App Store"> "Preferences," and then select "Automatically download apps purchased on other apps."

Reinstall the software

If you open or delete an app purchased with your Apple ID, you can reinstall it.

1. In the App Store on your Mac, click your name on the left-hand side, or if you're logged in, click "log in".
2. Find the purchased application you want to re-upload and click the "Download" button.

You can download the application from the Website and upload the application from the CD. See Uploading and Uninstalling Applications.

Save on Windows and Mac

When you open an application or Finder on your Mac, a window on the desktop will open. Only one application can be processed at a time; the name of the application (boldly displayed) and the application directory are displayed in the database.

Every application (such as Safari and Mail) allows you to open multiple windows or different windows at the same time. macOS offers many ways to run open source applications and windows.

Move, align and join the glass windows

On a Mac, do any of the following:

- Move window: drag the top of the window to the desired location. Some windows cannot be removed.

- Fixing glass windows: drag the glass window in place of another glass window - when the glass window is close to another glass window, it will be closed without being screwed. You can put several windows on one side.

To make the glass windows the same size, drag the edge you want to enlarge again so that the edge is close to the edge of the adjacent glass window, parallel to the edge, and stand.

Attach the two windows on one side and align the windows on each other by pulling the edge of one window to the other side so that the

- Merge application windows into a tabbed window: In the application, select "Window"> "Merge All Windows".

Redo the page in a different window, select the page and choose Window/move Tab to New Window, or just drag the page out of the window. Learn how to use labels in Windows.

Increase or decrease the glass window

On a Mac, do any of the following in Windows:

- Expand window: when you click the green magnify button on the left-hand side of the application window, press the Option key. To return to the size of the previous window, press the Option key again and press the button.

You can double-click the title of the application to enlarge the window (while "Zoom" is set in the Dock & Menu Bar preferences).

- To lower the window: press the yellow lower button in the left corner of the window, or press Command-M.

You can set an option in the Dock & Menu Bar that minimizes the window when you double down on the title bar.

Most glass windows can be re-opened by hand. Drag the edge of the window (top, bottom, and sides), or double-click the edge to enlarge that side of the window.

Switch quickly between application glass windows

On a Mac, do any of the following:

- Switch to the first request: Click Write Press.
- Paper on all applications: press the Command key, press the Tab key, then press the left or right key until you find the query you want. Release the command key.

If you change your mind while scrolling requests and do not want to change requests, press the Esc (Escape) key or Period key, and then release the Command key.

Close window

On a Mac, do any of the following:

- Close a particular window: In the window, tap the red "Close" button on the left-hand side of the window, or press Command-W.
- Close all windows of the application: tap Option-Command-W.

Closing one or more windows of an application will not close or exit the application. To do this, click Command-Q, or click the name of the application in the desktop menu, and select Exit [App]. View application form.

You can hide the job request by pressing Command-H.

Use the Mission Tool to quickly arrange windows and spaces in one layer to easily see the windows and where you need them.

Use split-view apps on Mac

Many apps on the Mac support a "split view" mode, which allows you to use two applications per page at the same time.

1. On a Mac, move the cursor to the green button on the left side of the window, and select "Tile the window on the left of the screen" or "Tile the window on the right of the screen" the "screen" from the menu will appear.

2. On the other side of the screen, click the second application that you want to use.
3. In a separate view, do any of the following:
    - Move to one side: Move the cursor over the center separator, and drag left or right. Place in the main, double -click the split bar
    - Rotate the face: Use the window frame to drag the window to the other side. If you do not see the taskbar, click on the window and move the cursor on the screen.
    - Show or hide the hard drive menu: Move to or from the top of the screen.
    - Show or hide the Dock: Move to or from the Dock.
4. To stop using an application in isolation view, click on its window to display the menu bar, move the cursor to the green button on the left-hand side of the window, then select the entire window from the menu that appears or click the button.

The remaining applications will be expanded to the full screen and will be available for download. To stop using the entire screen application, move the cursor over the thumbnail of the screen and click the exit button that appears in the left corner of the thumbnail.

If you use an application in full protection mode, you can quickly select other applications to routinely perform isolated browsing on a wireless network. Press the Mana-i arrow (or swipe up with three or four fingers) to enter the power of the mission, drag the window from the power of the mission to the thumbnail of the defense application fill the space bar, then click "Split View" to connect the Sketch map. You can drag a thumbnail on top of another thumbnail in the horizontal space.

To use the request as a separate inspection at other police stations, ensure that the box "Monitor has a separate area" is selected in the Mission Department requirements.

Use the program in full screen on your Mac

Many apps on the Mac support full-screen mode (an application fills the entire screen), so you can use every single inch of the screen to work without disturbing the desktop.

1. On a Mac, move the cursor to the green button on the left-hand side of the window, then select "Enter Full Screen" from the menu that appears or click the button.

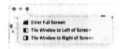

2. As a full defense, do any of the following:
   - Show or hide the hard drive menu: Move to or from the top of the screen.
   - Show or hide the Dock: Move to or from the Dock.
   - Move among other apps in full screen: Use three or four fingers to swipe left or right on the trackpad, depending on how you set your trackpad preferences.
3. To stop using the full screen, move the cursor over the

green button, and select the full screen from the menu to view or click the button.

Make the window larger without exposing it to the full length, enlarging (or moving closer) to the window. Move the indicator to the green button on the left side of the window, hold down the Option key, then select "Zoom" from the menu that appears or click the button. The glass window will be enlarged, but the land and Dock will be visible. To reset the size of the previous window, press the Option key and press the green button again.

You can double-click the title of the application (at the top of the application window) to expand the window. If the request is reduced to the Dock, change the name bar option in the Dock panel and menu options to "Zoom".

If you are using a full-screen application, you can quickly select another application to use the "split view." Press the Mana-i arrow (or swipe up with three or four fingers) to enter the power of the mission, drag the window from the power of the mission to the thumbnail of the defense application fill the space bar, then click "Split View" to connect the Sketch map. You can drag a thumbnail of the program into another thumbnail in the horizontal area.

Download Safari apps and offers from the App Store on Mac

To find the right app and extend Safari, search for it or browse the App Store. Once you know what you need, you can use your Apple ID to make purchases, or you can purchase a download code or gift card.

Find and buy apps

1. In the App Store on a Mac, do any of the subsequent:
   • Search for apps: Enter one or more words in the

search box on the left side of the "App Store" window, then click Return.

- Browse the App Store: Click "Discover", "Create", "Create", "Play", "Develop" or "Share" on the left side.

Applications designed for the iPhone or designed for the iPad are integrated with Mac computers and Apple devices. Learn how to use iPhone and iPad apps on Macs and Apple devices.

2. Click on the name or icon of a program to get a description, view customer statistics and reviews, and see the software's privacy features.

3. To apply, click the button indicating the cost of the application or "Receive". Then click the button again to install or purchase the app (or use Touch ID).

In the setup process, you can pause or pause.

Change your download and purchase settings

1. On a Mac, select "Apple Menu"> "System Prefers."
2. Click Apple ID.
3. Click Media and Sales (on a page).
4. Choose your option.

Purchase an iTunes gift card, Apple Music card, or discount code

- In the App Store on your Mac, click your name on the left-hand side (or "Sign Up" if you're not already signed up), then click "Reduce Gift Card" in the top right corner. Enter the deposit code or code on the gift card.

Inand your gift card has a box on the side of the code, you can use the built-in box on your Mac to purchase the gift card. After clicking "Redeem", click "Use Camera", and insert the gift card 4 to 7 inches (10 to 18 cm) from the camera. Make sure the code is located in the center of the preview area, and the card will be held until purchased.

See the Apple support article. What does a gift card mean to me?

Purchase in-app information and subscriptions

- Some programs purchase additional information, including software upgrades, game information, and subscriptions. To purchase in-app, enter your Apple ID (or use Touch ID). To learn more about subscriptions, see Manage Subscriptions on the App Store on Mac.

Download apps that have been purchased by other family members

If you are a member of the "Family Sharing" group, you can download eligible apps purchased by other family members.

1. In the App Store on a Mac, click your name on the left-hand side, or click "sign-in" if you're not already signed in.
2. Click the "Buy" menu and select a family member.
3. Click the download button on the product side.

To change the settings for downloads and purchases, select "Apple Menu"> "System Prefers"> "Apple ID", click "Media and Sales" on the page, and then select your choice.

Install and uninstall software package from a disk on the Internet or Mac

You can download and upload the application from the Internet or the CD. If you no longer need the software, you can delete it.

Install the software

On a Mac, do any of the following:

- For applications downloaded from the Internet: In the "Downloads" folder, double-click the disk image or package file (such as an open box). If the supplied organizer does not open, open it and follow the instructions on the chart

Note: If there is a discussion about installing apps from an unknown developer, see how to remove Mac apps from an unknown developer.

- For programs on CD: insert the CD into the CD drive on the Mac or insert the CD drive on the Mac.

To re-install an application downloaded from the App Store, please use the App Store. Check out the installation of products purchased from the App Store on Mac.

Uninstall the apps

You can remove downloaded and installed programs from the Internet or CD-ROM.

1. On a Mac, click the Finder icon in the Dock, then click "Applications" on the Finder page.
2. Do any of the following:
   - If an application is found in a file, open the application file to check if there is an uninstaller. If you see an uninstall [App] or [App] uninstaller, double-tap it and follow the instructions on the screen.
   - If there is no application in the folder and there is no uninstaller, drag the application from the "Applications" folder to "Trash (" (at the end of the Dock).

Tip: The next time you leave trash in the trash, the app will be permanently removed from your Mac. If you have files created with the program, you will not be able to open them again. If you decide to save the request, please download it before unpacking so you can select the application in the trash and select "File" > "Restore".

Open downloaded apps from the App Store, use the launchpad.

Privacy and security

Protect your privacy on Mac

Privacy is a serious problem in the use of applications to transfer information through the Internet. macOS includes security features that can improve your privacy and prevent the amount of information about you and your Mac from being disclosed via the Website.

Use protection time

You can use the "Screen Saver" to monitor your child's use of computers and control their exposure to websites. Find out what the defense time is?

Select the "Apple" list of options> "System Prefers" and tap "Screen Time".

Use custom features in Safari

Safari offers many features to help you control privacy on the Web. You can view it privately, so Safari doesn't keep a record of the sites you visit or what you download. You can block pop-up windows, prevent websites from storing cookies on your Mac, and more.

Restrict any personal information you share with the app

With the help of location services, applications such as websites can collect and use information about your location. You can turn off location services, or you can choose apps that can view information about your location.

Some apps can collect and use information from your contacts, photos, calendars, or memories. Some applications may include a microphone or keyboard on a Mac.

- See more topics:
- Permit apps to see where your Mac is
- Restrict the image to the image

- Avoid accessing your relationships
- Prevent access to the list
- Hold the image in the clipboard
- Prevent access to paleo

Choose whether to share analytical information

You can support Apple improve the superiority and performance of its products and services. macOS can collect analytics data from the Mac and send it to Apple for analysis. The information is only sent with your consent and then sent to Apple anonymously. Learn how to share knowledge with Apple from a Mac.

To choose whether to send analytics data to Apple, use the "Privacy" section of the "Security and privacy" options.

Select the "Apple" menu> "System Prefers", click "Security and Privacy", click "Privacy", and then click "Analysis and Improvement".

Adjust the firewall

You can use a firewall to protect your privacy by preventing inappropriate internet communication with your Mac. If the firewall is enabled, you can use "incognito" mode to prevent your Mac from being seen by others on the site. See Using a server to block communications with Macs.

To set up and configure the firewall, use the "Firewall" button of the "Security and Privacy" settings.

Select the "Apple" menu> "System Prefers", click "Security and Privacy", and then click "Firewall".

Find out what's blocked from finding you in Safari on your Mac

When you visit a site, you can see what's been blocked from finding you.

1. In the Safari app on the Mac, enter the name or URL of

the page in the "Smart Search" field.

2. Click the "Privacy" button in the taskbar.

For "Privacy profile", which displays a list of known trackers that are blocked from finding you, select "Safari"> "Privacy profile".

To start blocking browsers, see how to block web searches in Safari.

Find the app in "find My" on Mac

In "Find mine", you can see where the missing device is and play a sound on it to help you find it.

Important note: To find a lost device, you must add "Find my device" before it is lost.

Verify the location of the device

1. In "Find my app" on your Mac, tap "Anything".
2. In the device list, select the device you want to have
   - If the device is available: Show it on the map so you can see its location.
   - If the device cannot be found: Under the device name, "Location not found" is displayed. If you want to be notified when a location is available, click the "Info" button on the map and select "Notify availability." After setting up, you will receive a notification.

Play sound on iPhone, iPad, iPod touch, Mac, and Apple Watch

1. In "Find my app" on your Mac, tap "Whatever thing".
2. In the "System" menu, select the device you want to play the sound on, and then click the "Information" button on the map.
3. Click to play sound.

Note: You can hold down the Control key and press the player in the list of items, then choose to play a sound.

- If the device is online: the sound starts and sounds after a short delay, then plays in about two minutes. The device may vibrate. The "See my [device]" alert will appear on the device's dashboard.

An email will be sent to your email address with Apple ID.

- If the device is offline: The sound will play the next time the device is connected to a Wi-Fi or internet connection.

For information about using "Find My Info" on other devices, please visit the user guide for your iPhone, iPad, iPod touch, and Apple Watch.

Play sound on AirPods

1. In "Find my app" on your Mac, tap "Anything".
2. In the "Internet" menu, select your AirPods, and then click the "Information" button on the map.
3. Click to play sound. If your AirPods are separate, you can press "Left" or "Right" to see them at the same time.
   - If your AirPods are online: They will immediately play a sound (for 2 minutes).

An email will be sent to your email address with Apple ID.

- If your AirPods are disconnected: The next time your AirPods are in the middle of one of the devices and the "Find My" app is open, you'll get a notification on the device.

To learn more about using "See my stuff" on AirPods, please see the AirPods support website.

Prevent the device from making noises

If you see a game and want to finish it before the sound stops, do one of the following:

- Mac: tap "OK" on the "Find my Mac" display.
- iPhone, iPad, or iPod touch: Press the power button or the volume button, or the "Ring / Mute" button. If the app is locked, you can either unlock it or swipe to close the "See my [app]" alert. If the app is unlocked, you can click "OK" in the "See my [app]" alert.
- Apple Watch: Click "Off" in the "Find My Watch" button, or click the Digital Crown or Side button.
- AirPods: Place the AirPods in the box, then close the lid, or click "Stop" on "See me".

Get screenshots on the app

1. In "Find my app" on your Mac, tap "Whatever".
2. In the "Site" menu, select the device for which you want to find the path, then click the "Information" button on the map.
3. Click on the path.

Note: You can hold down the Control key and click the app in the list of items, then select the direction.

Open the "Maps" app and show a route from your location to the location of this app. See directions on the map.

Tip: You can help your friends find their app by opening iCloud.com so they can access their iCloud account on a Mac. In the "People" menu, select yourself, then click the "Information" button on the map. At the bottom, click "Peer Help", click "Use an Apple ID", and then release your friends.

Manage cookies and web information in Safari on Mac

You can change the preferences to Safari's preferences and allow Safari to retain cookies and web data.

In the Safari app on your Mac, select "Safari"> "Preferences", click "Policies", and then do one of the following:

- Prevent viewers from using cookies and site data to influence you: Select "Prevent site searches".

Cookies and website data will be deleted if you do not visit and interact with the tracker's website.

- Always block cookies: select [Block all cookies].

Websites, third parties, and promoters cannot store cookies and other data on your Mac. This may prevent some systems from working properly.

- Always allow cookies: deselect "Block all cookies".

Websites, third parties, and advertisers can store cookies and other information on your Mac.

- Clear cookies and stored data: Click the database browser, select one or more browsers, and click Clear or Clear All.

Clearing the data can reduce the search, but you can leave the site or change the service.

- View sites that store cookies or data: Click to save site data.

Note: Modify or disable them in other requests including cookies and web browsing in Safari.

Restrict the image to the photo gallery on the Mac

Some applications and websites can use your camera to take pictures or videos. You can decide which applications are allowed to use the camera on the Mac.

1. On a Mac, select the Apple menu> "System Prefers", click "Security and Privacy," and then click "Privacy."
2. Select the camera.
3. Make sure the check box is next to an app that will allow it to download your camera.

Uncheck the checkbox to finish downloading this program.

If you cancel access to an app, you will be asked to search again the next time the app tries to use your camera.

If you allow third-party applications or websites to use your camera, each of the information they collect will be under their language and privacy policies. You are encouraged to be aware of the privacy practices of the related pages.

For system administrators who need information about deployment security settings, please refer to the Mac Deployment Reference.

Reset your Mac login password

Sometimes you need to reset the login password — for example, if you've forgotten the password and can't use the password to remember it.

After resetting the user's password, a new permanent keychain will be created to store the user's password. Learn more about keychain terms.

Use your Apple ID to reset your password

If you connect a user account with an Apple ID, you can use the Apple ID to reset the password.

1. On a Mac, select the "Apple" menu> "Restart", or click the "Control" button on your computer, and then click "Restart".
2. Click on your operator account, click the question mark in the password field, and then click the arrow next to "Reset it with your Apple ID."
3. Enter an Apple ID and password, and click "Next".

Follow the instructions to reset your password.

Use the recovery key to reset your password

If you enable FileVault encryption and create a recovery key, you can use the recovery key to recover your password.

1. On a Mac, select the "Apple" menu> "Restart", or click the "Control" button on your computer, and then click "Restart".
2. click your operator account, tap the question mark in the keyword field, and then click the arrow next to "Reset it with retrieval key."
3. Enter the recovery key and press next.

Follow the instructions to reset your password.

Reset passwords for other users

The administrator can share the passwords of other users.

1. On a Mac, select the Apple menu> "System Prefers" and then click "Users and organizations."

If the lock is on the left side, click on it to open the desired side.

2. Select a user and click "Reset Password".

Set security on Mac

You can take more measurements to record your Mac.

Use a strong password

To ensure the security of your information, you need to protect your Mac with a password and choose a password that is not easy to choose. Find tips for creating vocabulary and learn how to use the words.

Require user login

If other people can access the Mac, you will need to set up a separate user account for each user using the Mac and require each user to access it. This prevents non -users from using the Mac. It separates user files, so users can only download their files and settings. Users will not be able to view or edit the files or settings of other users. Learn how to organize users, visitors, and groups.

Secure your Mac when not in use

If the Mac doesn't work for a while, you can configure the Mac to leave the current user. Make sure your Mac is unused. You will need to ask for a password to wake her up or a security guard. See Ask for a password after waking up your Mac. For convenience, you can set a hot corner to press if you want to quickly lock the screen. See Use the hot corner to start the screen saver.

Limit the number of navigation users

One or more people can have executive rights on a Mac. By default, the administrator is the first to configure the Mac.

Administrators can create, maintain and delete other users; install and uninstall software; and change settings. For these reasons, the administrator must have a standard user account to use when administrator privileges are not claimed. If the security of a typical user is broken, the risk is greater than that of a user with superior responsibilities. If many people use your Mac, please limit the number of users with upper privileges. Learn how to organize users, visitors, and groups.

Use FileVault to manipulate data on Mac

If you have personal or private information on your Mac, you can use FileVault encryption to prevent that information from being seen and copied. FileVault stores information stored on the Mac, so if the password is not entered, it will be locked and unreadable. Please see how FileVault encryption works.

Protect your Mac from malicious software

Many features of macOS can help protect your Mac and your personal information from malware or malware. A common way to advertise malware is to include it in an unsolicited request.

You can reduce this problem by only using software from trusted sources. By setting the "Security and privacy" options, you can specify the purpose of the software being installed on your Mac.

1. On a Mac, select the Apple menu> "System Prefers", click "Security and Privacy", and then click "General".

If the lock is on the left side, click on it to open the desired side.

2. Select the resources to allow the program to install:
   - App Store: Only apps are allowed on the Mac App Store. This is the safest setting. Apple will see the developers of all applications on the Mac App Store and review each application before approving it. macOS checks the software before opening it for the first time to make sure it has not been fixed since it was released by the developer. If there is a problem with the app, Apple will remove it from the Mac App Store.
   - App Store and known developers: Allow applications to the Mac App Store and applications used by experienced developers. Developers who are known to be registered with Apple can choose to submit their application to Apple for security checks. If there is a problem with the application, Apple can revoke its license. macOS checks the software before opening it for the first time to make sure it has not been fixed since it was released by the developer.

Other types of files are not protected, apart from applications. Scripts, web files, and Java files can damage your system. Of course, not all files are safe, but you need to be careful when opening similar downloads. If you are trying to open these files for the first time, a path will appear. See open requests that override security settings.

Use Personal Browsing in Safari on Mac

Using the "Personal View" window will not protect your personal information, and sites you visit will not be shared with other users.

Open the custom glass window

- In the Safari app on the Mac, select "File"> "New Custom Window", or change a previously used Safari window to "Custom Window". The window that uses "Search Engine" is a dark "smart search" field with the word white.

You are using the "Personal Accounts" window:

- Searching for one class is separate from a search that starts in another, so the site you visit cannot track your browsing over several seasons.
- Web pages you visit and autocomplete information will not be saved.
- The web pages you open are not saved in iCloud, so when you view open pages from other apps, these web pages will not be displayed.
- Using the "Good Searches" field, your most recent searches are not included in the results list.
- The item you download is not included in the download list. (These things always stay on your computer.)
- If you use the "Switch", the "Private Browsing" window will not be provided on your iPhone, iPad, iPod touch, or other Mac computers.
- Changes to cookies or website data are not saved.

Web sites cannot change the information stored on your device, so the services available on those sites may be different until you disable the "Personal information" feature.

Note: none of the above conditions apply to other Safari windows that you open that do not use "Personal View".

Always use personal surveillance to open windows

1. In the Safari app on your Mac, select "Safari"> "Preferences" and click "General".
2. tap the "Open Safari" pop-up menu, then select "Have a personalized browser window".

If you don't see this option, select "Apple"> "System Prefers" menu, click "General", and then make sure to select "Close window when request exits".

Prevent personal viewing

- In the Safari app on the Mac, close the "Browse Problems" window and change to another window that doesn't use "Personal Search", or choose "File"> "New Window" to open the window. the glass that does not use "Safety Key". To improve privacy:
  - Delete all downloaded items using the "Search" window.
  - Close the "personal search" windows that are always open to prevent others from using the "Back" and "Forward" buttons to find the pages you are looking for.

Out of use and by using the "Search Search" window, you can navigate to cookies and data stored on all sites and avoid searching across sites.

If you forgot to use the "Independent View" window, you can clear your browsing history.

Sign up with Apple on Mac

Signing up with Apple is an easy and personal way to access apps and systems. It uses your Apple ID to securely create accounts with apps or apps — no need to fill out forms, verify email addresses, or choose new passwords — and it's easy with that. this yes.

The button labeled "Sign in with Apple".

Create an account for an application or website

1. On a Mac, when asked to create an account for an application or website, click the login button and continue using Apple (if you have one).
2. Follow the instructions on the chart, keeping the following numbers in mind:

   - If you do not want to use your real name, click the "First Name" field and enter a different name.
   - If you have multiple emails related to your Apple ID in the Apple ID requirements, please select the email address you would like to use for this application or site.
   - If you want to keep your email private, click "Hide My Email". Apple will issue an email address and a special email address that is used to send emails from apps or systems to your actual email address.

Log in to your application or website

1. On a Mac, click the login button and continue using Apple.
2. Enter the login password on the Mac (you must enter the Apple ID password), or, if the Mac has Touch ID, use Touch ID.

You can sign in from other devices (iPhone, iPad, Apple Watch, and Apple TV) using the same Apple ID to sign in.

Change the address used to send emails from apps and websites

If you decide to hide emails when you create your account, and there are numerous email addresses associated with your Apple

ID in Apple ID favorites, you can change the address where you receive emails. sent.

1. On a Mac, select the "Apple" menu> "System Prefers" and click "Apple ID".
2. On the sidebar, click "Name, Phone, Email", then click "Edit" after "Hide My Email".
3. Select another email address and click Finish.

Use the Apple settings of the software or system to change the login

1. On a Mac, select the "Apple" menu> "System Prefers" and click "Apple ID".
2. On the next page, click "Passwords and Security," then click "Edit" after "Apps that use your Apple ID."
3. Click on the program or website on the landing page, and then do one of the following:
   - Close the email forward: Click Error. You will no longer receive emails from this application or site
   - Stop using Apple: click "Stop using Apple ID". The next time you try to log in to use the software or website, you will be asked to create a new account.

Learn how to use passwords on a Mac

macOS wants to give you a more stable computer. Mac security lies in the use of strong passwords in critical areas.

Login password

The login password (also known as the user password) allows you to log in and access data on your Mac. Creating a password, remember the password, write it down, and keep it safe. Rights are limited by user type. Administrators are required to perform many important tasks, such as setting up system requirements, configuring applications, and maintaining common users. Learn how to organize users, visitors, and groups.

Apple ID

Apple ID allows you to access the iTunes Store, App Store, Apple Books, iCloud, FaceTime, and other Apple services. He has an email address (e.g. michael_cavanna@icloud.com) and a password. Apple recommends that you use the same Apple ID for Apple services. Creating an Apple ID password, remember the password carefully, write it down, and keep it safe. If you forget your password, you can use your Apple ID to reset the password. Log in to your Apple ID account page.

Password on iCloud Keychain

Finding passwords can be very difficult, especially if you are not the best user to use the same word twice and get many apps. iCloud Keychain currently stores Wi-Fi passwords and passwords on Mac, iPhone, iPad, and iPod touch. It can store account passwords and settings that you add to web browser preferences on your Mac to this day.

When you need to create a new password for a site, Safari recommends using a hard-to-use password and keeping it in your iCloud key. Safari only loads it the next time you need to log in, so you don't have to remember it or install it on any device. To create passwords for websites and Web applications, you need to use strong passwords provided by Safari. See Use iCloud Keychain ensure information security.

If you do not use the required strong password and need help with the password later, please refer to the website help or website statistics.

If you would like to help with the password of a request linking to the Website or an account on the Website, please review the documents that came with the request or the website information that supports the request. . For example, if you have a mailbox with your service or website, please check the documentation online or contact the provider. Please see Apple's support article, if Mail on Mac continues to ask you to enter your password.

The password when entering the keychain

Keychain stores passwords for various applications and services. This saves you the hassle of entering a keyword for each item on the keychain. The keychain password protects your key, which will be unlocked when you log in. Learn more about keychain terms.

Healing key

FileVault uses to manipulate information on the Mac, you can create a recovery key. If you have forgotten the password, you can use the recovery key to unlock the start bar and change the password. The recovery key does not need to be stored in the same location as the Mac where the Mac is located.

Use the keychain to navigate passwords on the Mac

macOS uses the Keychain to help you track and protect passwords, numbers, and undisclosed information that you use daily on Mac computers as well as iOS and iPadOS apps.

You can use the "Keychain Access" application on your Mac to identify and store your keychain. Using iCloud Keychain, you can update passwords and other security information across the device.

What's the key?

A keychain is a decrypted container that can securely store your Mac's account usernames and passwords, applications, servers, and systems, as well as confidential information, such as credit card numbers. credit or account PIN codes.

When you visit websites, email archives, webinars, or password-protected sites, you can choose to keep the password on the keychain so you don't have to remember it. and enter the password from time to time.

Each user on the Mac has a login keychain. The password to enter the keychain is the same as the password you used to access your Mac. If the administrator on the Mac has reset your password, you will need to reset your hard disk password.

Get a Keychain

You can use the "Keychain Access" application on your Mac to view and store your username and other keychains, as well as items stored on the keychain, such as keys, keys. credentials, passwords, account information, and memos. If you forget your password, you can find it at "Keychain Access". Learn more about keychain integration.

iCloud keychain

If you use iCloud, you can create an iCloud keychain to securely store internet login and credit card information used with autofill in Safari, as well as Wi-Fi network information. iCloud Keychain stores this information today on all Mac computers as well as iOS and iPadOS apps. iCloud Keychain also keeps track of the accounts you use in "Mail", "Contacts", "Calendars" and "Messages", so it can be used on all devices. Learn more about iCloud Keychain.

Tip: Using passwords and credit cards on the web, you can ask Safari to store them in the keychain and fill them out for you. If you're using the iCloud Keychain on Mac, iOS, and iPadOS apps, Safari can populate the information stored on all devices. Find life-saving credit cards.

Music, news, photos, and more

How to Pay with Apple Pay in Safari on Mac

You can use Apple Pay to make purchases easily and securely on your Mac in Safari. Check Apple Pay while watching, and then use a Mac with Touch ID, iPhone (iOS 10 or later), or Apple Watch (watchOS 3 or later) to complete the purchase. If you use your iPhone or Apple Watch to complete the purchase, you need to log in with the same Apple ID as your Mac.

Note: Apple Pay is not available everywhere.

Before using Apple Pay, please set up a credit or debit card on the device used to complete the purchase.

1. In the Safari app on the Mac, in the options, click Apple Pay.

You can change your credit card, email address, or contact information before completing the purchase.

2. Complete the purchase.

- Mac with Trace ID: Place your finger on Touch ID to complete the purchase. If the contact ID has not been set, you can tap the "Pay" button on the screen and enter the password. If you don't have a Trace Bar or you're using a Mac with Apple Silicon, you can double-click Touch ID and enter the secret code.

Only one user account on the Mac can use Touch ID on the Mac to complete Apple Pay purchases. Other user accounts need to use iPhone or Apple Watch.

- iPhone: Double-click the side button, and then

use Face ID for authentication on the iPhone or use Touch ID
- Apple Note: Double-click the page button.

Play songs from your music library in "Music" on your Mac

Listen to music the way you want-use the controls in the "Music" window to recreate songs, change how they are played, and more.

Ask Siri. Languages like this:

- "Play a song"
- "What song is this?"

Learn how to ask Siri.

1. In the "Music" app on your Mac, do any of the following to view the songs in your music library.
   - To view songs or albums: Click on each option under "Library" on the left. For example, click on an album to view all the songs in your media library.
   - Select a list: Select a list below the list on the left page.
   - Search your music library: Browse and search for songs.
2. Move the cursor to one or more songs, and then click the "Play" button.
3. Do any of the following:
   - Shuffle and recreate songs
   - Use new game line
   - Play songs accurately
   - Done between songs
   - Prohibit playing songs
   - Love or don't like this song

You can listen to songs from the CD. Check out the Cēdē wall.

Download and play Apple Arcade games on your Mac

When you sign up for Apple Arcade, you can download and play games on your Mac and any supported applications.

Note: Apple Arcade is not accessible in all countries or regions.

Download games

1. In the App Store on your Mac, click Arcade on the sidebar.
2. Search or watch games.
3. Select the game and click "Find".

The game has been downloaded to the application file on the Mac. Available on the launchpad. See the launchpad to view and open applications.

The game you downloaded remains in the "Applications" folder, and then delete it.

Play a game

Even if you are not connected to the Internet, you can play downloaded Apple Arcade games on your Mac at any time.

1. On a Mac, tap the Launchpad icon in the Dock (or use Strip Control) to open Launchpad.
2. tap the game you want to play.

Note: Fixed hardware and software are required. There may not be any knowledge everywhere. When the service is available, not all information is available. the Apple support article "Accessibility of Apple Media Services".

Leave the game

- When playing Apple Arcade games on your Mac, press Command-Q.

Wash the game

1. On a Mac, click the Launchpad icon in the Dock (or use Strip Control) to open Launchpad.
2. Click and hold the game you want to delete until the application icon starts to shake, and then click the "Delete Game" button.

Apple Arcade games also support Game Center. In the "Game Center", you can see the games your friends have played and their achievements. Please check the Apple support article to get Apple Arcade game data on all devices.

Create recordings on Mac

Use voice memos and use your Mac as a voice recorder. Use a built-in microphone, supported headphone jack, or external microphone for recording. You can use the same Apple ID to listen to your voice memo recordings on devices registered in iCloud. See iCloud settings.

1. In the Voice Memo program on your Mac, click the "Record" button (or use safe mode).
2. To pause, click the "Pause" button. To continue, click again.
3. When finished, click Hana in the lower right corner.

Your recording will be saved under your local name (if "naming based on naming" is selected in the preferences) or the name "naming".

After saving the recording, you can choose to play it and edit it, such as renaming and deleting.

Basics of image editing in "Images" on a Mac

You can use the "Photo" editing tools to make simple changes to the image, such as rotating the image or cropping the image to get the best possible combination. You can use twelve sophisticated editors to change the look and color, remove marks and stains, remove red-eye, change the white balance, and more.

For more advanced editing, you can use the "Level" and "Curve" controls to adjust the brightness, contrast, and tonal bands of different areas of the image. Find out how to match photos and request photo editing. You can enhance and edit real-time videos and photos. Learn how to edit and improve video and live graphics.

Images in the edit view with the editing tools in the "Edit" button on the right.

When you are editing a photo or video, "Photo" saves the original image, so you can always discard the changes and return to the original view.

The changes you make to the photo or video will be reflected everywhere in the office, including albums, projects, and more. If you would like an image or video to have a unique feature, and that feature appears in one version of the program, please first copy and make a copy.

Edit photos or videos

1. To take photos on your Mac, do any of the following:

- Double-click the image or video thumbnail, then click "Edit" in the action box.
- Select the thumbnail or video thumbnail and click Return.

2. Do any of the following:

- Zoom or play the image: Click and drag the "Zoom" slider.
- Make edits: Click Edit to display the editing tools. Learn to adjust lighting, display, and so on. The picture.

- Request filters: Click a filter to display filters that you can apply to change the look of the image and video. See Use filters to change the appearance of images.
- Capture: click "Crop" to display options for capturing photos or videos. See the fruits of the Land correctly.
- Rotate images or videos: Click the "Rotate" button in the toolbar to rotate the image. Keep clicking until you get the direction you want. Press the Select key and press the button to locate the image on the clock.
- Auto enhances photos or videos: Click the Auto enhance button to automatically adjust the color and contrast of photos and videos. To undo the changes, press Command-Z and click "Revert to Original".

3. To end the editing, click "Finish" or click "Return".

Editing photos or videos, you can click the arrow keys to change the rest.

Make copies of the images

Create different versions of photos or videos, copy them, and edit the copies.

1. In the "Photos" program on your Mac, select what you want to copy.
2. choose "Image" Copy 1 Image" (or press Command-D).

If you want to copy a photo, click "Copy" to insert the video clip, or click "Copy as still photo" to paste the photo only.

Compare photos or videos before and after editing

Editing a project, you can compare the edited power with the original power.

1. In the Photos app on your Mac, double-click the image or video to open it, and then click Edit in the Action box.
2. To view the original image, press and hold the "No Ad-

justment" button, or press and hold the M key.

Release the button or the M key to view the product and edit the information.

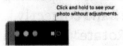

Make a copy and paste

After editing a photo or video, you can copy the edits and paste them into other projects. You can only click edits one item at a time.

Note: You may not copy and paste settings through the retouch maker, redesigner, cropper, or third-party extensions.

1. In the "Photos" program on your Mac, double-click on the product you want to edit, and then click "Edit" in the taskbar.
2. Select "Image"> "Edit copy".
3. Double-click the item you want to make edits to, and then click "Edit".
4. Select "Image"> "Image Image".

You can hold down the Power key and press anything on check edits, then select "Copy Adjustment" or "Paste Adjustment".

You can quickly erase changes to photos or videos. Open the last change you made, choose Edit> Open or press Command-Z. Discard all changes and start over, select the object, and then select Image> Find Image Image.

Tips and tricks

With macOS Big Sur, Apple has redesigned the entire macOS UI to be redesigned with both the iPhone and iPad. At first glance, the Mac-like Dock icon may surprise you, but the wide application with a high-resolution screen and a translucent panel is probably the reason for the great design. Apart from this, there are many new features of macOS Big Sur — you can check out the list of best features here. You can easily use the tips and tricks on your MacBook Air, MacBook Pro, or iMac. Now that macOS Big Sur is available, introduce it below.

macOS Big Sur is an update that brings new features and user changes. At first glance, please take a moment to make changes to the system, as these changes may change. You can read these summaries of macOS Big Sur tips to learn how to best use the OS.

Release the control switch

The navigation system plays an important role on the iPhone and iPad and has been seen on macOS Big Sur. But where? Just click on the "Moke Center" icon on the top right of the screen (as if the two sliders are placed on top of each other) and it should pop quickly.

Not surprisingly, macOS Big Sur Control Center has borrowed a lot of money from partners on iOS and iPadOS. You can easily configure Wi-Fi, Bluetooth, AirDrop, hassle, and other built-in restrictions. There are some sliders for adjusting the brightness of the screen and the sound.

Most of the constraints will increase to reflect the other options. For example, clicking on the "Brightness" button will bring up the option to access "Darkness" and "Night Shift".

Pull the server to the hard drive bar

The server is a new add-on, but you do not need to install it every time. If you want to quickly access control, simply drag it from the "Control Center" and enter the control panel. Then stay there.

For example, you can add flash controls to the desktop navigation bar and quickly access all available options.

Quickly edit notifications

macOS Big Sur comes with an improved ad server. As with iOS and iPadOS, notifications are integrated with the application, and they are easy to service.

Even better, you can navigate notifications directly. Just click on the notification or advertisement of a specific request. Then, select "Send Quietly" to send notifications to the "Notification Center" quietly in the future. Alternatively, click "Close" to cancel future notifications from the application.

Additionally, you can click on the "Advertisement" option for in-depth advertisement control.

Quickly adjust the size of the widget

The ad server has the same new widgets as it does on iOS 14 and iPadOS 14. They lack compatibility (e.g. the "Calculator" widget is only deeply connected to the "Calculator" app), but most of them offer exact compensation.

In addition, most of the apps on macOS Big Sur are resizable, allowing you to quickly switch between specific levels. Right-click on the app and select any available size (small, medium, or large).

Percentage report

After upgrading to macOS Big Sur on your MacBook, you will soon see the missing percentage in the Battery icon in the hard drive menu.

If you would like to refund, please go to the "Prefers System" first. Then click Dock & Menu Bar> Battery. Check the box next to Percentage.

Show the life of the remaining batteries

With the release of the macOS Sierra (before 2016), Apple has released the "remaining time" reading of the MacBook screen. Fortunately, it's back on macOS Big Sur. Just click on the "Battery" icon on the main menu to see the estimated value of the rest of the batteries on your MacBook.

Review the user history of the file

macOS Big Sur provides detailed statistics using the MacBook tablet. Go to "System Prefers"> "Battery" to check the battery level and "screen usage" for the last 24 hours to 10 days.

If you are using an iPhone or iPad, you should be very familiar with this screen ("View"> "Battery"). However, you will not be able to see the electricity usage statistics by applying them on your Mac. All being well this will upturn in the future.

Change the tone to multicolor

macOS Big Sur allows application developers to implement their custom colors. Comes with a new theme color scheme called "multicolor". Go to "System Prefers"> "General" and click the "Accent Colors" radio button on the far left to switch between multiple colors.

After this process is complete, the application will display the different color schemes as determined by the developer.

Remove the sticker in Windows

If you despise how apps are "plugged in" into the background card (while using dark mode), then you'll be glad to hear that macOS Big Sur can protect you from doing so.

Go to "System Prefers"General" and uncheck the "Allow color coding in Windows" option.

Customize Safari labels

On macOS Big Sur, you'll see the biggest improvements in Safari. Not only does it run much faster (50% faster than Apple's browser), but it also has a new user interface, support for the WebExtensions API (allowing developers to add ports from other web browsers), as well as cool new features (like the first look at the label.

Better yet, the new tab page is customizable. Clicking the "Customize" icon (similar to a bunch of sliders, located in the lower right corner of the screen), allows you to use or disable new tabbed pages, such as "Favorites", "Frequent visits", "Personal information", etc.

Amazingly, you can add backgrounds to newly-selected tabs from a set of built-in backgrounds, and add your images. Apple's great honor allows us to add something sexy to Safari.

Website translation

Safari has a native function that converts web pages from popular languages to English. When you visit a foreign site, just click on the "translate" image in the text box to redirect to the page.

You can download both iOS 14 and iPadOS 14 versions of Safari.

Check for blocked browsers

Safari on macOS Big Sur can not only prevent web browsers from regularly displaying your logins, but it can also detect logins in real-time. To browse a website, simply click on the "Policies" icon to the left of the address, and a window with a list of blocked trackers will appear.

In addition, you can provide full personal information about the last 30 days by clicking anywhere in the "Legacy" section in the new tab. If you do not know this, please use the "Personalization" menu to access it.

Watch YouTube in 4K

Apple now supports the VP9 codec, which means you can watch YouTube in 4K in Safari. So, if you've used Chrome (or any other browser) before, now is the time to go back to Safari.

After uploading a 4K video on YouTube, just visit the "Good" menu and select the 2160p or 2160p60 option to convert the stream to 4K.

Create and send Memojis

The Messages app has been improved on macOS Big Sur, and its functionality is similar to those on the iPhone and iPad. As a result, you can use memes, GIFs, and message results when iMessaging with other people. Click the App Store icon on the side of the text site to get started.

Fixed conversations in letters

The email app allows you to pin conversations, making it easy to retrieve your favorite messages. To do this, right-click on a conversation and click "Pin". You can have up to 9 conversations.

Consistent answers and comments

In a group discussion, you can respond directly to specific messages. This will trigger the "Messages" request to open a new level (below the main response), making it easier to track responses later.

However, don't forget to use keywords when replying — type @ [nickname]—to point the message to a specific person.

Attach fixed notes

The Notes application on macOS Big Sur has an improved search engine and improved text marking. Otherwise, it will remain unchanged, as there is a new option to attach permanent notes.

For example, if you have a lot of hard notes, you can quickly retrieve the remaining messages. Just use the "fold/show" icon at the top of the "save" section to hide/open the list.

Adjust the vividness of the image

The "Photos" app on macOS Big Sur has made subtle edits to take in an immersive experience — for example, the new mock-up looks like a photo booth. It can use machine learning to get better results using one-click tools, so don't forget to give it a try.

Plus, there's a new "Vividness" slider that allows you to adjust the vividness of the image. In "Edit" mode, add "options" below the "color" section to display it.

Start video editing

With "Photos" software, you can not only view videos but also do more. You can access all pre-saved editing options for images. Switch to "Edit" mode to try them out.

Look around the map

In the end, the Maps app caught up on macOS Big Sur with similar apps on the iPhone and iPad. In addition to selected guides, indoor maps, and shared E.T.A.s, you can explore the surrounding area. To share an area, click "View around" (if available) to move around the city's streets in 3D.

If you use an iPhone or iPad, you need to get used to it. However, Mac's large screen makes it all the more familiar using a deep "look around".

Plot electric cars and bicycles on a map

The Maps app organizes the navigation of electric vehicles in a breeze, which allows you to easily train E.T.A.s by considering the exact location. In addition, the map has detailed landmarks that can display information such as elevation and slope for better planning.

Do not switch hands-on AirPods

When you use some AirPods, they automatically switch between iPhone, iPad, and Mac. So the next time you start listening to any music on your Mac, you don't have to bother with a Bluetooth keyboard to connect to AirPods.

At the time of writing, this feature is available in macOS Big Sur Public Beta. When the board hits the shelves in late September or early October, they should be available.

Give things to work on memories

In aesthetic terms, the "memory" app is no different on macOS Big Sur. But you get a lot of positive rewards. Now, it irritates you with ideas of the day and time the tools are working, provides an improved search function, and the ability to re-edit or hide lists intelligence, and more.

But one of the most important things is a new model that allows you to share what you've done with others. During or after creating a task in the shared list, click the "Information" button and add the search name to the "Assign to" field.

Improve the quality of voice memos

The Voice Memo application on macOS Big Sur is much better at setting up voice memos. It comes with smart files, can easily organize your sounds, and also gives you the ability to create your own.

There is a very new feature called "praise recording". Go to the "Edit Record" screen of the message, and then click the "Enhance

Record" icon on the top right of the screen. This reduces back noise and improves sound quality.

Complete automated system updates

Our automatic system downloads possible? but why? macOS versions often take a while to complete, right? no longer. macOS Big Sur supports fast updates that start in the background and run in the background, so downtime is minimized.

If you dare, please go to "System Prefers"> "Software Changes" to enable automatic updates.

macOS Big Sur — a new experience

Yes, men, that's all. We hope this tip can help you get ready for macOS Big Sur. Of course, the upgrade isn't necessary for everyone, but there is a huge demand switch from Intel to Apple components. At the very least, macOS Big Sur should achieve greater stability in the Apple ecosystem in the future. But what do you think? Finish quickly on the comments page below.